11

YEARS
OF
NAPPIES

SIMONE PHILLIPS

11
YEARS
OF
NAPPIES

CHOOSING TO LIVE
INTENTIONALLY

INSPIRED
PUBLISHING

11 Years of Nappies
Choosing To Live Intentionally
First Edition, First Impression 2021
ISBN: 978-1-77630-668-8
Copyright © Simone Phillips

Published by:
Inspired Publishing
PO Box 82058 | Southdale | 2135
Johannesburg, South Africa Email: info@inspiredpublishing.co.za
www.inspiredpublishing.co.za

The stories in this book reflect the author's recollection of events. Some names, locations and identifying characteristics have been changed to protect the privacy of those depicted. Dialogue has been recreated from memory.

Table Of Contents

Dedication

I want to dedicate my book to a few people who have not only impacted my journey but also loved and supported me throughout.

To God, my Heavenly Father

If it had not been for Him, I wouldn't have been able to write this book. God really moulded me in my twenties for this moment right here, and I am beyond grateful. Some days were not easy, I felt like I was being squeezed and couldn't find my breath, but somehow God would send someone my way or allow something to happen for me to allow me to catch my breath. God's hand was there every step of the way. Thank you Lord for moulding and making me who I am today.

My late father-in-law, Allen Conroy Phillips.

Born on the 30/11/1953 departed from us on the 13/01/2021.

Dad, thank you for being a solid and strong human being. Thank you for leading the way where we can now walk and do better. Thank you for always being as straight as an arrow and not holding the punches; your honesty was such an incredible trait to have, your very own superpower. We miss you daily, especially your witty sense of humour. You were a giant of a human being and the true definition of a man. I love you Dad and will forever be honoured to carry your name and continue your legacy by handing over the batons to our children as you did for both Rob and me.

To my Husband, Robert D. Phillips

RD, thank you for loving me during the highs and the lows; thank you for never letting go of me no matter the storm. Thank you for pushing me, encouraging me, and motivating me on the days I wanted to give up. Thank you for believing in me more on days when I didn't believe in myself. Thank you for loving me from the lost and insecure girl to the woman I am today. Thank you for allowing me to be true and authentic to myself and for not wanting to change me. I love you from my soul R, and I will forever be by your side.

My Beautiful kids.

King, Ethan, Micaiah, Zoe, and Eden.

Mom loves you more than anything in this world. Because of you guys, I am. You are my home. You are where I reside. I am so blessed and honoured to be your mom. I thank God for choosing me to be your mother; I wouldn't have it any other way. Let my story show you and teach you, it's not how you start, but it's how you end. Don't ever allow anything or anyone to set you back; go get what you want and sometimes it means you would lose people, but follow your dreams. Be relentless and persistent in following your dream. Your father and I will always be there to love and support you guys. Good and bad times; we got you. Always. Thank you for making me a better human being. I love you guys unconditionally throughout infinity. Love Always.

This right here would not be possible without you all.

Track 1

Shackles

Take the shackles off my feet so I can dance, I just want to praise you.
What ya want to do? I just want to praise you, (Yeah, yeah)
You broke the chains now I can lift my hands. (Uh feel me?)
And I'm gonna praise you. (What ya gon do?) I'm gonna praise you.
In the corners of mind, I just can't seem to find a reason to believe.
That I can break free, because you see I have been down for so long, feel like the hope is gone, but as I lift my hands, I understand.
That I should praise you through my circumstances.

SONG BY MARY MARY

CHAPTER 1

Bloodline

I was born on 3 May 1984 and I am one of the five children in our family. I am from a strict, Christian family where we attended church services habitually and the Christian values were built into each of us as children.

Ours was not a family free of dysfunction; I grew up with my fair share of dysfunction, sibling rivalry, moving from one house to another, changing schools and not being taught social or communication skills.

I do not know much about my parents' childhood, but it is fair to mention that they grew up during the apartheid era and they gave what they could although the tide of injustice was against them. It was a system that did not give them social and economic opportunities.

One thing that is still vivid in my memory about my childhood is the death of my sister who was my brother's twin. Although I was young and couldn't fully comprehend the loss or pain, I could see the pain my mother was going through. Therefore, I experienced loss from a young age and some of the things we lost include homes, which was so traumatising because a home defines your world as a child. When you are a child, you never understand huge change because no one sits you down to explain things. Numerous things happened during my upbringing and the pace with which they unfolded did not afford me the time to understand and process the changes. I just had to move with the tide.

Certain people were supposed to be at the centre of my life but they were not. I never knew my dad's family or much about his upbringing. I saw my grandmother approximately four times in my lifetime and I don't think she even knew my name.

One thing I know without a doubt is that my dad had a heart for people. He always helped people in need at church, in the community and even family members. He always did it without hesitating and people loved him for this.

My mother was a prayer warrior who interceded for many people. People always called on her to pray for them and that commitment made people love her. In the church, she was also a preacher and through her sermons she led many people to salvation.

Outside our home, my parents were well respected, but at home, their relationship was frosty. I cannot remember a day when they told each other that they loved each other or showed some affection.

My relationships with my siblings were never close. We had sibling rivalry; my sister disliked me from a young age. As a result, I suffered abuse from quite a young age, but I have no idea why she resented me. She would want to beat me up at every chance she got. She was mean to me and wanted to cause me pain, whether it was physical or emotional. She always said I was my father's favourite, but I disagree. I guess because of my personality; being an affectionate person, I showed that love and affection to my dad without realising this was his love language. A love language describes how we receive love from others. It is: words of affirmation (saying supportive things); acts of service (doing helpful things); receiving gifts (giving gifts that tell a person that you were thinking about them); and affection (showing love) was my dad's love language and he appreciated it.

I didn't know that loving my dad would result in my mother completely disliking me. She would say hurtful things to me for no reason and get me into trouble with my dad by lying to him about me. This resulted in me getting a beating from him. I was a child, so I could never dare correct or challenge my parents; I simply kept quiet.

This tumultuous relationship with my parents made me a tomboy. It kept me away from home; the less time I was at home and in my mother's presence, the better. I was never taught about a menstruating cycle, boys, sex, cooking, cleaning, being a wife or being a mother. I remember in our home, if our parents were fighting, my mother expected us children to choose her side, and that meant you did not speak to dad for as long as she did. She taught us that it was ok to disrespect my father when she was not ok with him. I never supported this or picked a side. I figured

13

that I was a child to both of them, as a result, my mother's dislike for me worsened. My mother allowed us to be rude and disrespectful toward my dad if they were having a disagreement, but we would not dare if they were ok. I could not understand this.

The age difference between my siblings made it so difficult to forge close relationships with each other at any given age because we hardly had anything in common. My two older sisters were close because there are two years between them, so these relationships my siblings formed made me feel excluded, displaced, and not wanted.

When my brother was born, I was five and was excited because I believed I would also have a friend, but the age difference just didn't allow it although we did many things together. Five years later, when I was ten, my youngest sister was born. The age gap once again was too big for us to even try to bond. As much as my dad was closed off, he was my safety net. I would go home when I saw his yellow Caravelle bus coming down the street.

I attended three different primary schools because we moved from one house to another, but I was so happy that I attended only one high school. When I was in high school, my relationship with other family members didn't get any better. My relationship with my mother simply deteriorated and my dad's absence didn't help matters; he was at home less and less. When my eldest sister moved out, we never saw much of her. Moreover, my second eldest sister fell pregnant at the age of nineteen, which left the house cold. All these developments made me to feel displaced and unwanted.

I started dating a guy who didn't live far from our church. We had to sneak around to see and talk to each other because we both knew that my dad would kill both of us if he found out about our relationship. Having this secret affair was fun; he was an ok guy, but I was so naïve. It wasn't a smooth relationship, so we were on and off because I always heard rumours about him dating other girls.

At the age of sixteen, when I was in Grade Eleven, I started getting flattering letters from James, the father of my cousin's baby. He would hand the notes to his sister who in turn handed them to me. By the time I got his second letter, I was involved in a horrible car accident and was in hospital for months and missed two terms of school. I was involved in the accident during the week, a day after I had finished exams.

When the accident occurred, we were on our way from Johannesburg city centre to fetch my brother from school. In the car was my sister, who was driving; my friend at the back seat behind the driver's seat; my niece at the back, with no seat belt, and; me on the front passenger seat. A speeding car skipped a red robot and rammed into our car. Seconds before the accident, I had unclipped my seatbelt to take my then one-and-a-half-year-old niece from the back to the front because she was crying to sit with me. Amazingly, on this particular day she did not want to sit on my lap; she went straight to my feet and that saved her because the impact would have killed her.

The second she sat down, we were hit and I instantly went blank. I was told the impact was so severe that my friend who sat behind my sister who was driving was thrown out of the car and had multiple injuries. Fortunately, she did not lose her baby since she was pregnant at the time. My sister injured her chest, ribs and fractured her ankle. The impact of the crash flung me through the windscreen and I fractured my neck in three different places. I was unconscious for a number of days and when I finally regained consciousness, I heard a doctor who stood over me saying he did not know how I had made it out of the accident alive and not paralysed. He said had I kept my seatbelt on, the impact would have snapped my neck. At the age of sixteen, I knew there was a God and that He had a plan for my life.

I was in hospital for almost four months, unable to walk, or do anything for myself. I had a traction drilled into my skull to keep my neck still. That time made me conscious of God; I knew He had me and every morning I would cry while thanking Him. I had to undergo intensive physio to help me walk and balance again. Everything was off; I couldn't even wear closed shoes and my memory was fuzzy. To this day I can remember certain things about that period of my life, but not everything. I missed out on half of my Grade Eleven school year, but I worked extra hard in the last term to make up for lost time and I passed the grade. My accident realigned things for me, as young as I was; it made me realise that God had a plan for my life. I had to learn how to walk, I had to show determination and not give up. It was challenging at times, but I had to push through. I realised my strength there.

When I eventually got back to school, everything was an adjustment. I couldn't wear closed shoes and during my time away I had won a netball award one which I've always wanted. My parents did not tell me this wonderful news.

I started seeing more and more of *James in the mornings and afternoons at school; he was seriously pursuing me. He and my cousin had broken up and were co-parenting. He was upfront, open, and honest about his feelings and I agreed that we could date. We dated, but tried to keep our relationship discreet until we were ready to let people know about it, but I guess people - especially at school, started noticing that he was always around.

News of our relationship quickly spread and reached my dad's ears. One day *James and I were at a petrol station and my dad suddenly pulled up, he took off his belt and started beating me in public. The more *James tried to stop him, the harder he hit me. I eventually managed to break loose from his grip and run home. My mother and sister were home; I was in pain and was crying trying to explain what had happened. My dad came into the lounge and just continued beating me, both my sister and mother couldn't stop him. He didn't ask questions, didn't say a word, he just hit me with the buckle of his belt. I was sixteen at the time and at some point during the beating I stood and peed on myself, the pain was completely unbearable. When he finally decided to stop, he instructed me to go to bed. I could not bath that night; I just had to obey and go to bed.

I woke up the next morning with ugly bruises all over my body, and I was in so much pain. I could barely walk, but had to go to the bathroom on my own to wash off all the blood from the previous night's beatings. I had to open my wounds and see to myself; no one was there to help me. My mother did not even come to check up on me; all she said was that I got what I deserved.

That week I did not go to school because had people seen what I looked like, my dad would have probably gone to jail or been reported to child services. No one asked me what had happened, how I felt, or how I was doing. The family never spoke about that day.

*James and I continued seeing each other. One Sunday, our house phone rang and it was my cousin's mother wanting to speak to my mom. She was asking if my mom could come and see her. My mother, my older sisters, and I went to *James's house and met with his mom, my cousin's mom, my cousin, and *James. I was accused of all sorts of things and my mom kept saying the relationship between James and I was wrong and my dad was very upset about it and did not want to hear anything about it. I never expected what happened next.

*James stood there in front of everyone and told them how much he loved me and that he wanted a relationship with me and that I had not done anything wrong. That moment was the first time in my life that someone had defended me, stood up for me, and loved me enough not only to say it, but show it. Most people walked away from that meeting very angry, but I was happy. As much as everyone wanted to make our relationship look bad and wrong, we did not look at it that way. Again, my mom never asked how I felt; we simply didn't talk about it.

I continued my relationship with James despite all the criticism. Our meeting place was my sister's place on weekends. She was very supportive of our relationship.

By this time I was in Grade Twelve and there was no doubt that my boyfriend would be my date for the Matric Dance. We co-ordinated the colours I wanted.

On the day, James called me throughout the day to check in on me and how everything was going; I was so excited. He was supposed to meet me at my sister's place at 18:00, but suddenly his phone was off from 18:00. I called his number endlessly and so did my sisters, but there was no answer. He did not pitch; he did not even send a message to say he couldn't make it. Here I was, on probably the most important night of my school years with no date and in tears. I was so hurt and disappointed but couldn't allow James's no-show to ruin my night.

I called my ex; he and I were still friends. I didn't harbour any ill feelings toward him and man, he didn't even hesitate. He drove to get his suit, didn't ask me any questions, and was just a perfect gentleman. I would always be grateful to him for stepping in and turning my night into a fun and memorable one. Furthermore, I never heard from *James or saw him again. I never received an explanation or apology from him, just complete silence, but later, I heard that he made up with his ex and was getting married.

My relationship with *James taught me that if someone loves me enough, they would fight for me (not physically).

Going through all this at a young age taught me a lot. I started finding my voice and began to stand up for myself and my brother to both my parents. The beatings stopped, but I remember I was told to move out of the house during my Grade Twelve prelim exams. I had to suck it up, focus, and write my exams. I started clubbing and drinking with my sisters. When the results were released, I had passed my matric and to celebrate this achievement, I went out clubbing with my sisters and got extremely drunk. The celebration did not end well though, because I fell extremely sick and the sickness made me loath alcohol to this day. I swore that I would never drink again and that is exactly what happened. I stopped drinking but continued going out and clubbing with my sisters. I would spend my weekends at my sister's place, which enabled me to go out clubbing and that's where I met *Jessie; in a club.

I would say *Jessie was my first serious boyfriend. I say this because he was mature and four years older than I was. He came home to ask for my parents' permission and blessing to date me. This man so happened to be one of the biggest gangsters in the south of Johannesburg at the time; almost everyone knew him, and as a result everyone knew I was his girlfriend. I was looked after, driven around, showered with gifts and respect. We dated for a while, but we were on and off until I ended things with him at the age of twenty. The relationship taught me what I did not want in a union. I am so grateful that even though I was so naïve, none of my ex-boyfriends ever abused me physically, emotionally, or mentally.

The first twenty years of my life were not a smooth drive. I had to deal with a lot, sometimes not even dealing with challenges, but just moving on. The experiences taught me that I don't have to settle or continue with what has been given to me. I realised the strength and determination I had. I figured out that I am a black-and-white person; I have no grey areas.

Ever had a feeling of intense pain? Pain so intense that it feels as if your body is suffocating, as if your heart is being squeezed, as if your soul is pierced over and over again? Well I did. This is how I felt when I was in my twenties; it was the space I was in. Let me tell you about that space. The first twenty years aligned and prepared me for the years ahead.

Lessons Learnt

- You are not what you are told.
- You don't have to continue the cycle.
- Find your voice and break the cycle.

Track 2

Humpty Dumpty

And so, if ever you see Humpty Dumpty or anybody else who
— who's had a fall; please tell them that He's mending broken
pieces
And He'll be there to fix it all.

SONG BY BEBE WINANS

CHAPTER 2

Being

2004, I was twenty years old. I got my first permanent job in the financial services space, moved into my own place, and slowly started finding my corner. This is where I met my person; my husband; Robert Phillips. We did not click from the onset; it definitely was not love at first sight from my end, but Robert says he saw me and said to his friend David, "She is a super rocker."

Robert has always been a very competitive and persistent person. He was always the number one, always the top agent, always winning accolades till today, as a result everyone knew him. Everyone, especially women loved him. At the time of meeting Robert, I was in a relationship that was nearing its end because I had outgrown it and needed more.

One morning at the office canteen, I walked in to grab some coffee and Robert was there with his colleague and he said, "Simone, can I pick you up tonight, and we go out for a film or something?" I thought he was joking, laughed it off and said, "Yes, sure we can." I didn't think he was serious. I went home, got comfortable, listened to music, and while I was reading a book, my phone rang. It was Robert asking if I was ready. I laughed and said I wasn't. He said he was on his way, so I quickly got ready and waited for him to arrive. It was our "unofficial official" first date; we watched a film, Troy, and went for coffee afterwards.

During coffee, we got to know each other, and I saw a different, softer side of Robert. He told me he was a single dad of a two-year-old boy, and he was no longer with his son's mother. He was very open and honest and so was I. He later dropped me off at home and I was impressed with him. From there the relationship developed; he was doing the things that I needed in a relationship without me having to say a word.

Later on, I met his family and his son; *King. The family welcomed me warmly. They all seemed so friendly, but I wasn't always sure about how to be with *King. I had no idea what he expected of me. I had no idea what I had to do and what I couldn't do. These were conversations I never had with Robert. He never made me feel as if there was an expectation, but I could never talk about what the expectation was when I knew I was dating a single dad. I was like Humpty Dumpty, happy and comfortable until I had my great fall.

I guess news of me meeting *King and Robert's family got to *King's mother, *Charmaine. Never did I expect a whirlwind of events that followed. One afternoon after work on our way to my place, we bumped into *Charmaine and her mother. I had never met her before, so this was a first and before he could properly introduce me to them, she said, "Is this the kaffir you left me for?" I stood there in complete shock and disgust. I simply walked away and as I walked away, the insults and vulgarity that followed had me speechless; little did I know that was only the beginning. Thereafter, she would call my office causing all kinds of havoc and chaos. I was so embarrassed, but Robert always reassured me that he had me.

November 2004, Robert and I found out we were pregnant, little did I know that my relationship would take a turn for the worse. No one was happy about the pregnancy. Robert did not want me to be alone during my pregnancy, so we decided to move in together with *King. *King was at a good school, and he could see his mom every weekend, but boy, it was an uphill battle. His mother would come and cause chaos at the gate of our home; she would pitch up in the early hours of the morning or just call in the early morning hours saying Robert must come fetch his son. She made a habit of this and it became more and more unbearable and frustrating. I realised that she was so used to everyone dancing to her tune, but I was not having it. Every time I would mention it, Robert and I would end up fighting.

That's when the abuse began. I would always confront him about the disrespect and inconvenience that came from her end and demand to know why he tolerated it.

It's as if when *Charmaine heard about my pregnancy, it amplified her disrespectful behaviour. This made things worse in our relationship because the physical abuse started happening and later became frequent. I will never forget the first time Robert slapped me; I was pregnant and man, did I cry? I cried myself to sleep that night. It was a shock to my system because I had never been there. Everything about my life at the age of twenty was unfamiliar and scary.

2005 July, our eldest son was born. I went into early labour because of all the stress I had been going through. At the hospital, I had my parents visit and no one from the other side of the family came. The question they asked was: "Is he black?". As a new mom, it was so hard; I battled physically, emotionally, and mentally. I never felt like I had real support. Robert was there, but he was not present.

We got married in December 2005, but things got worse. On the day before our wedding, *Charmaine and her mother called to threaten and tell me that the wedding would never happen and that Robert was still very much in love with *Charmaine. No one was happy that we were getting married. We had no support from both sides of the family, therefore, we ended up paying for our wedding ourselves.

Things with *Charmaine simply escalated. At this point, our marriage was an absolute mess; the conflicts easily degenerated into frequent physical fights to a point where I started fighting back. I was only good enough to buy *King things and to do certain motherly duties that his mother completely failed to perform, but I could not discipline him. The minute I did it, a war would break out from Robert's family and *Charmaine. I was just not given a fair opportunity with *King; I was never encouraged, supported, or even guided on how I had to deal with him. People just criticised and insulted me all the time.

Robert started acting out. He started coming home late, staying out with friends, drinking, and lying about giving *Charmaine money. This caused even more fighting. I moved back home countless times, but Robert would simply apologise and make promises that he knew he would not keep. The marriage was extremely volatile; we were both angry, frustrated, but not communicating properly. One day I took all *King's clothes and threw them on the kitchen floor. I told Robert to take *King back to his mother since I could never do anything right in everyone's eyes and Charmaine was the best mother to her son. This resulted in a huge physical fight and argument.

Amidst all this turmoil, we decided to buy a home.

*King was in a good school and our eldest child went to the same school. We both had good jobs and lived a good life, until *Charmaine found out about our second pregnancy. All hell broke loose. She did not have our home address, because we were building our family and didn't want her interfering with our kids. I would meet her at a McDonalds when I went to drop off or collect *King, but she was never happy. She would want to know why Robert was not coming. One of Robert's family members decided to give *Charmaine our address and boy, was it a mess? She came to our gate and started screaming and shouting at our eldest son. It didn't end there, she opened a kidnapping case against Robert saying she wanted her son. Unfortunately, the law is never for a dad, no matter how good he is, so she won the case and took him. It was hard losing *King because she took him out of a stable home, a good school, and away from family and friends to an unstable environment.

A couple of days later, she had the South African Police Service (SAPS) come to our home while I was four months pregnant to have me arrested for Gross Bodily Harm (GBH) on a minor. She had a doctor friend write up a report saying I had abused *King. Some pictures were attached to the report. I spent a night in a cell while I was four months pregnant. The Oxford Dictionary defines a jail as a building where people are kept as a punishment for a crime they have committed or while they are waiting for trial.

I spent a night in a jail cell while I was four months pregnant. And It was a rather difficult pregnancy. My fingerprints were taken, I was shaking non-stop and crying hysterically. I could not believe that a person would go to that length to simply get what she did not want. The cell I walked into to spend the night was dingy, dark, empty, and the smell was horrible.

There was another lady in the cell with me, but we didn't say much to each other. I was hungry because my last meal was breakfast and it was evening already. I didn't get anything to eat, no water or anything to drink; I didn't even have my tablets that I was supposed to take twice a day. Furthermore, I couldn't use the toilet because it was dirty, messy, blocked and the odour was overpowering. I was also hesitant to use it because I knew that I would get an instant bladder infection if I tried; I didn't want to take that risk. I slept on a gym mat without a blanket. Well, I didn't sleep. I cried endlessly and asked God why this was happening to me.

The morning finally came and Rob was there early so I could change clothes. I got into the back of a police van like a real criminal. When I peered through the small window of the van, tears just rolled down my cheeks non-stop. I couldn't stop the flow of my tears even walking into court.

I was placed in a small room with other prisoners waiting for our names and cases to be called. Eventually, after a long wait, my name was called. As I walked to the box, tears kept flowing down my cheeks. I was asked to confirm my full name and surname, the charge against me was read, and the judge gave me bail.

At that moment we didn't have the money for bail; who always has money handy in case they get arrested? Definitely not me. I couldn't speak to Rob to ask what we would do, but I just knew he would get it sorted. As we sat in the room waiting for bail to be paid, a police officer walked in and announced: "All those who got bail, your bail must be paid by 12:00pm, if not we will take you to Sun City Prison with the rest of the prisoners." Immediately I started to panic and stress; suddenly I felt this intense pain in my lower abdomen. I knew something was not right. I had not eaten, or drank anything. I had not even taken my medication and I had cried all night and all morning. Right there in that room I said to God, "I refuse to lose my baby because of some person's evil nature." I refused. I begged God to keep him safe and to get me through the trying time.

Time was ticking and the police officer came again at 11:30 and he told us that we would be leaving in thirty minutes. I noticed that one of the ladies who were seated opposite me had a phone. I got up and asked her if I could use her phone to call Rob and I promised to buy her airtime once he arrived.

Without hesitation, she agreed to let me use it. I called Rob in panic and told him what the officer had said. Rob said he was on his way, but he had to drive to Sandton to his mother's office to get the money. I burst into tears and all that could come out of my mouth was: "Please hurry!" and I dropped the call. Again the officer came in and told us that we were going to leave in ten minutes. My heart dropped.

As the officer turned around to leave, my name was called and there was Rob. He held me so tight, I sobbed uncontrollably. I couldn't speak, we got into the car and drove to the gynaecologist's office. We sat in the car for a few minutes, all Rob kept saying is: "I am so sorry; I am so sorry." I will never forget that scene. At that moment, "It's Ok" by Bebe and Cece Winans started playing and the words felt so real and so meaningful; the lyrics were for me. We went up to the gynaecologist's office and he did an ultrasound and checked me. I couldn't talk, Rob answered all his questions and told him what happened. He put me on bed rest for almost two weeks, increased my medication doses, and told me to take it easy. I was just so happy to hear the baby's strong heartbeat and to know that he was well.

*Charmaine showed no remorse for what she had done. We appointed a team of attorneys because we took the charges very seriously and I was going to defend myself. Eventually, *Charmaine dropped the charges because she could see I was very serious about defending myself against the flimsy charges and I guess she knew the doctor she and her mom got to second the charges could end up losing his medical licence. There was no way he could prove the allegations in a court of law.

Again, throughout this traumatic ordeal, no one called or texted me to check up on me or my son; I still had no support. Once again people took *Charmaine's word and believed her lies. No one bothered to ask her why she dropped the charges if she was really telling the truth. I was just wrong once again, but that was always the case. I was the scapegoat for people to use when they needed to deflect their wrongdoings and shortcomings when it came to *King.

I did not leave *King; I tried my best with what I was handed, but I was expected to be *King's mom on *Charmaine and her family's terms. They wanted me to do things when and how they wanted me to.

*Charmaine had never kept a job for more than a few months; most of the time she had been unemployed. She did not know what it meant to get up on a good or bad day to make sure her kids had what they needed. She would use and manipulate people to get what she wanted. She was often unemployed and taking *King from Rob was an opportunity for her to get money. *King became her cash cow and she would milk people for all she could. By doing this, she used *King as her pawn. She went as far as lying to the clerk of the court and took Robert up for maintenance. For seven years, we were in and out of court with her. This was such a difficult period for us because Robert's department was going through a re-structuring and he was not earning the salary that he used to anymore and I had just given birth to our second son in August 2007. All this greed and mess made us lose our home. Did she care? No, not at all. She depleted our medical aid funds and showed no concern for our kids. To worsen our woes, she kept going back to the court to request an increase in *King's maintenance. Man, this was a very difficult time for us to get back on our feet.

We still tried to do what was best for *King. I even offered to help her with her second baby. We bought baby formula and nappies because both she and her partner were not working. I extended my help because the baby would wiggle and cry a lot, and she did not know how to bath, feed, or do anything for him. Despite the show of support with her baby, she once again took Robert up for maintenance.

This was probably one of my lowest moments and I started praying *Charmaine away. I told God that I couldn't bear it anymore. I had tried everything I could, but Charmaine did not appreciate my efforts. I was done. For seven years I prayed day in and day out for God to remove her from our lives and seven years later, He did just that. To this day she is completely out of our lives. We've heard many stories of what has happened to her, but we don't really know which one is true. The only sad thing is that *King had to suffer for the decisions of his mother. He lost an opportunity to have a relationship with his father.

*Charmaine was ruthless, heartless, and selfish and she stopped at nothing to get what she wanted. The amount of money she wanted was too much for us and we ended up moving in with Rob's sister.
I would never forget what *Charmaine put me through.

*Charmaine tried to break me, break my family, and most importantly, destroy my husband. Yes, at times she thought she had won but she did not win the battle because ultimately the battle was not ours to win. This battle belonged to God and the minute I gave it to Him, it ended. Our family made it and today we stand only by Grace. I hope one day she will come to a place of peace where she will be accountable and responsible for all she has done. That season and its experiences unleashed the warrior in me and allowed my super power to come through. I am grateful for the learning experience.

To my stepson *King. I want to take this opportunity to apologise to you as I am one of the adults in your life who failed you. I should have done better. I should have fought harder. You have been and will always be a part of me. Even if you and I will never have an opportunity to sit and talk, I pray that one day you will afford your dad a chance to sit with you and talk to you about his experience and what he went through. Hopefully one day you will hear his side of the story and not build your life based on a one-sided narrative.

Your father and I love you more than you know; we've only ever wanted the best for you. We never wanted to unsettle you. We have had countless days of tears with you in mind, conversations about "what if" and "maybe we should have".

People can lie to you about many things, manipulate situations and even bad-mouth both me and your dad, but one thing they will never be able to change is that Robert Phillips is your dad. You are his and his blood runs through your veins. The truth always has a way of coming out and it will. When it does, we will be here waiting for you.

I pray that you will be blessed beyond measure and continue to grow into an incredible and strong man. I love you. I choose to not use your real name because of the sensitivity involved and to protect you.

Lessons Learnt

- People will sabotage you without you knowing.
- Sometimes you need to stand up and allow your voice to be heard.
- You need to know when to walk away.

Track 3

I Found Love

When I found you, I found the rest of my life. When I found you, I told all others goodbye. When I found you, I saw my fears fly away like a dove. When I found you, I found love. When I found you, I found the rest of my life. When I found you, I told all others goodbye. When I found you, I saw my fears fly away like a dove. When I found you, I found love. When I found you, I found my fate in your arms. When I found you, I found no cause for alarm when I found you, I knew this love was a gift from above.

SONG BY BEBE WINANS

CHAPTER 3

Parenting

Growing up, I always prayed that I would be married and have my kids in my early twenties. Little did I know that I would be having four in that period. That is exactly what I got.

At the age of twenty, I fell pregnant with our eldest son, who was born naturally in 2005; pure perfection. I was beaming with pride and love, but at the same time had to deal with the fact that I had no family support. I had no choice but to figure out motherhood and literally learnt as I went along. Man, I failed many times and yes I got it wrong, but one thing I knew deep down in my soul was that I loved my son with my very being. I just never felt like I was the best mom. I felt as if I was not present with my eldest son in his early years because I had so much to deal with and so many things were thrown at me from different directions.

At twenty-three, we had our second son born via C-section in August 2007; pure perfection. It was not the easiest delivery; it took me six weeks to recover. I remember I couldn't get off the bed for weeks on end. Every day before Rob left for work, he would make sure I had hot water in a flask, tea, coffee, sugar, a sandwich packed, a snack and water because I could only make it to the bathroom and no further. We still had no support and the fact that our second born was a breast-only baby until he was one year didn't make things easier. He wanted no one, not even Rob. No one could babysit him. He would cry non-stop to a point where his bottom lip would turn blue. I had no choice but to leave my job when he was four months to stay home with him until he was ready for people. Still, I was not a present mom. I was an emotional wreck, but I knew I loved him with my very being. At one-and-a-half, he decided to leave our room and became more independent.

At twenty-five, while on a contraceptive, I had to see a doctor for a terrible stomach bug. This came after I accidentally consumed a disinfectant at the office, yes by accident. The doctor put me on a scan to check if there was any internal damage, and there she was. I was twenty-one weeks pregnant; yes that is five months. Man, I cried. The doctor had to call Rob from the consultation room to console me. I cried all the way home, Rob looked at me and said he was giving me a week to cry and deal with my emotions but after that it was done, because we were having a baby and we had four months to get things done. That's exactly what I did: cried. Now, I didn't cry because I didn't want the baby, I cried because our second eldest was so demanding and dependent on me and in December 2008, we gave all things baby related away because we just wanted a baby break before we tried again. I guess God had totally different plans for us because here we were in the doctor's rooms in January 2009, and we got the news.

I had gained a whopping eighteen kilograms during my second pregnancy and I was in a terrible space, mentally, emotionally, and physically. Furthermore, I had never believed women when they said they did not know they were pregnant until I experienced it with this pregnancy. I had just become one of those women. Likewise, I had a menstruation cycle and I was finally losing weight but that was short-lived. In May 2009, our first daughter was born via C-section. Pure perfection.

At twenty-eight, on a contraceptive. My menstruation cycle was late, and I am not one to be late, yes a day or two late or early but not a week. I told Rob and he immediately said he would buy a pregnancy test. I was convinced I was not pregnant. He brought home the test and I took it and yes, pregnant. Me. DENIAL. I said to Rob it couldn't be; the pregnancy test must have expired. He made a deal with me and said he would buy a few more tests and if they all gave the same result, we deal with it and move on, and Bobs your uncle, all the tests were positive. Yes, I did. I cried. I said to God, "Can I have a break? You know we don't have any support and it is hard, Rob and I are struggling, our marriage is drowning, family is talking, and I am a total mess." In June 2012, our second daughter was born via C-section; pure perfection.

While in the delivery room, my body went into total shock and my blood pressure dropped. This was the first delivery where Rob was right next to me, whereas with the other births he watched the birth and cut the umbilical cords. This time around he asked not to see me like that. I lay there with tears running down my cheeks and I said to God: "I cannot do this anymore. This is the last. I am tired." At that moment I said, "Lord if you want me to have any more kids, please send Jesus down to earth to have a face-to-face conversation with me because He and I would need to talk". My body told me it was done. And I told God I was done! Rob and I never got to experience having family in the ward after our kids' birth with congratulations balloons and a room filled with love and smiles. It was and still is just the two of us.

Rob was there for every doctor's visit, however many there were. He witnessed the birth of all four of our kids and cut umbilical cords of three of them. One thing I can say without a shadow of a doubt is Rob was and still is an amazing dad to our kids. He was and still is a great support; we have mastered the art of tag-teaming with the kids. He has changed nappies, taken a night shift, made bottles, helped with the teething years, even helped with the potty training and the sick days. To this day, we are still a tag-team and we understand how intense and draining it can get and that makes it easy to give each other time out. It has become easier because the kids are older now.

In raising our children, the support never came. Rob and I did it. We raised four incredible human beings, yes with many struggles, many tears, many losses, many "we couldn't afford" moments, many "we didn't have" moments, many moments of family talking about how many kids we have, people looking at you like, "Are you crazy?" but we've also had many countless highs, many beautiful moments, loud laughter, and proud moments.

The struggles and lack of support have made me the mother I am today; the fearless and protective one. Man, I love my kids fiercely and deeply and will protect them no matter what. They come first, no one will ever make them feel second-best.

Those struggles brought out my superpower; I love hard. And man, do I love my beings? If I could wrap them in bubble wrap to protect them, I would. I could have stayed the same not present mother, but I refused. I did better because I wanted better.

A few years ago we took the kids out for dinner and I decided it was important for me to apologise to them for failing them; for not being a better mom to them. I had to because sometimes we as adults feel we don't have to explain or apologise to our children and I didn't want that. I apologised to them and I could see it meant so much to them and Rob did the same.

Growing up and to this day, my parents have never apologised to me about anything; they have never shown or taught me to be accountable and responsible. They did not teach me to say, "I am sorry. I apologise." I battled with this thing in my twenties and found it extremely hard, but I had to make the choice to change it. By me taking accountability and responsibility for the role I played in their lives and apologising for my wrongs, I am teaching my children that saying sorry is ok; that adults can be wrong; adults can make mistakes, and no one is perfect.

Furthermore, I absolutely refuse to raise broken and hurt adults. I need whole and solid adults. My squad knows without a shadow of doubt that I love them and that I've got them no matter what. They know whether they are right or wrong, I got them. I am their home; their place of safety.

My kids have made me want to be a better parent than what I had. They made me want to hand over good, healthy batons to them. They made me a better human being and it is my privilege and absolute honour to raise Ethan Dugan, Micaiah Kethan, Zoe Michal, and Eden Zyon Phillips.

The meanings of their names were very important to me when we named them because I needed to know that every time their names were called, greatness was spoken forth.

The meanings of their names:

Ethan is a name of Hebrew origin that means "firm, enduring, strong and long-lived". It appears eight times in the Hebrew Bible (1 Kings. 4:31, Psalms. 89 title, 1 Chr. 2:6 and 2:8.

Every time Ethan's name is called, we are calling forth firmness, endurance, strength and long life and that is what I want for my son.

Dugan; Is Rob's second name. It is Irish. Another word is "black".

Micaiah; The name Micaiah means "Who is like God?" And is of Hebrew origin. Micaiah was a prophet in the Hebrew Bible 1 Kings Chapters 20-22.

Which means every time Micaiah's name is called, we are calling for someone who is like God, which is what I want for my son.

Kethan; is a combination of both his brothers' names, Keli and Ethan.

Zoe; The name Zoe means "Life, abundant life." 1 John 5:12. Why do you think Zoe is used 125 times more than bios? Jesus doesn't want us to just live with breath in our lungs, but walking around as shells, merely existing. He wants us to have a rare vitality, experiencing the fullness of life, which means every time the name Zoe is called, we are calling forth abundant life and that is what I want for my daughter. Also, the way she came and the circumstances of us finding out about her were special.

Michal; It is a Hebrew name. The meaning of the name Michal is "Who is like God?"

Eden; the place where Adam and Eve lived before the Fall. Genesis 2:8–24. Any delightful region or Paradise. A state of perfect happiness or bliss. Delightful.

Which means every time the name Eden is called, we are calling forth delight, perfect happiness, and bliss and that is what I want for my daughter.

Zyon; We deliberately spelt it with a "y" instead of an "i". The name Zyon means Israel and is of Hebrew origin. In the Bible, Zion is a symbolic name of Jerusalem.

To my squad, let me start by saying, I am sincerely sorry for failing you, for disappointing and hurting you as a mom when I was younger. I dropped the ball and there is no excuse or a reason good enough in the world to ok that.

My vow to you guys is: I will always be there for you. I will always protect and guide you. I will always be your loudest, biggest, and most consistent cheerleader. I will always be there and nothing you ever do will make me love you less or stop loving you.

I will lift you up when you are down. I will be strong for you, and I will forever be the invisible woman - just like in the film Fantastic Four, who will protect and cover you.

You guys have healed my heart and made me a better human. Besides that, you are where I reside. The four of you are the reason I am.

You forever have a hulk right by your side and I will assemble when you need me to.

I love you forever.
I love you from my soul.
I will ride for these beings for the rest of the days.

Lessons Learnt

- Parenting is not easy, and therefore, you need someone who will work with you and make it easier.
- There will be people that aren't good for your children and their well-being, but you must choose your children every time.
- Do what is good for your children. Leave the past batons that were handed over to you and start your race afresh and hand good and healthy batons over to your children.
- Learn to apologise to your children; this teaches them that you too are human and as adults, we too make mistakes. Apologising is good for their mental health.

Track 4

Why I Love You?

I found love in you and I learned to love me too. Never have I felt that I could be all that you see. It's like our hearts have intertwined into the perfect harmony. This is why I love you. Ooh! This is why I love you. Because you love me, you love me. This is why I love you.
Ooh! This is why I love you because you love me. You love me.

SONG BY MAJOR

CHAPTER 4

Marriage

Inner ear conversations. Find your outlet.

1 Corinthians 13:4-8: "Love is patient, love is kind. It does not envy, it does not boast, it is not proud. It does not dishonour others, it is not self-seeking, it is not easily angered, and it keeps no record of wrongs. Love does not delight in evil but rejoices with the truth. It always protects, always trusts, always hopes, and always perseveres. Love never fails. But where there are prophecies, they will cease; where there are tongues, they will be stilled; where there is knowledge, it will pass away."

When one reads the above scripture, it sounds absolutely beautiful. This is exactly how you want your marriage to be; the bliss. Well, the first ten years of mine were the complete opposite. For ten years, I would cry asking God why I was there. I would ask God to remove me. The first ten years were more tears than anything else. I didn't know what it meant to be a wife; I had no real concept of marriage. I grew up in a household where I never saw my parents showing emotion. I didn't know that I needed to respect, honour, compromise, and depend on my person because I had not seen it and no one taught me those values.

December 18th 2005, on the day we said, "I do", I was twenty-one years old and Rob was turning thirty-one the next day. Yes, Rob is ten years older than me. It was a beautiful day that we paid for ourselves. Family either couldn't assist us financially or we were simply told an outright NO. We planned and paid for everything ourselves. I honestly don't think people and family were happy that we were getting married, but we did it. It was a beautiful day, but I had no idea what I was walking into.

A week after our wedding, Rob and I got into a massive physical fight. I sought help and advice from the elders in our family and was told the wedding should never have happened and that we didn't deserve to be married. In addition, they said Robert Phillips deserves nothing good in his life, so I should divorce him, ASAP. These are words I heard over a million times during the first ten years from different people: divorce him. However, for some reason, I couldn't take that advice.

For nine years of our marriage, the arguments were out of control, the physical fights continued, and got worse, and every time I would reach out I would hear: "Leave him", "Walk away" and "Divorce him". But again for some reason, I stayed. I loved this man; I loved my husband.

2007, while I was heavily pregnant, we joined our church, Crystal Ministries. We both walked out of the first service crying and saying, "This is a church and this is where we want to be." Don't for one second think the fights stopped. No. They escalated. We never missed a church service or a life group (home cell). The fellowship allowed me to find sense, direction and slowly gain strength. When we had our fights, I didn't speak to anyone. I completely withdrew from family and people. In 2008, we lost our home. Man; it was painful and we had no support in the midst of our own sand storm. We also had our car repossessed; that too was hard. Very hard. We felt humiliated and dehumanised. Rob had to start taking the bus at five in the morning so he could get to work and be back home at seven.

February 2009, six months pregnant, I remember at this time we were living in Rob's sister's garage; yes, with our children in a garage which was so small. It was a just one room, with a bedroom, kitchen, toilet and shower. Rob and I would sleep on the bed and the boys on the floor because I was pregnant. As small as it was, I would go on my knees right by the toilet and pray. I would pray until I had nothing left. Those prayers sustained us. We would be picked up for church on Sundays because we had no car and we would sit in church and wonder what we would have for lunch because we had absolutely nothing. We would go home having either jungle oats or my favourite to date, white porridge (mealie meal porridge). And yes, for Sunday lunch or during the week for supper too, while we had family getting together, having a barbecue down the road. I remember a time when we were down to nothing, waiting for UIF to pay out maternity benefits and I had no sanitary towels. I had to use toilet paper because we intended to use the little money we had to buy food, formula, and nappies for the baby. I sacrificed and used toilet paper, but never stopped praying.

A day later, Rob's sister asked if we needed anything from the shop, she would take us there and buy a few things. We went to the shop, and you know when the list of the needs is so long but the budget can only accommodate not even half of the list; that was us. We took what was of dire necessity because we only had a couple of Rands. While shopping, Rob's sister came over and said we could take what we needed and she would pay. I stood there with tears, but again we took what the kids needed; we did not even think of ourselves. She then came and asked me if I needed sanitary towels. I burst into tears and cried uncontrollably. Rob explained to her why I was crying.

That right there was God; nothing else. These were sore, painful, soul-piercing moments, but without realising it, they started building the warrior in me. We still attended Sunday services and never missed any. We attended our first marriage conference and man, lights started going on. We started realising that what we were experiencing in our marriage was exactly what God did not intend our marriage to be like.

2010 was the turning and tipping point. The make-or-break point for Mr and Mrs Phillips. The fights were still happening, but not as intensely as before. We realised our church had a family pastor and he could possibly help us in some way. I was so happy that we had found an outlet, a neutral person who was not going to judge us. We were both keen to have a peaceful union. Little did I realise this was paving the way for healing from that deep-rooted pain. We started our sessions with our family pastor, Pastor Neil. Our sessions were heart-wrenching and emotionally draining, but let me tell you, if it had not been for Pastor Neil, today I would be divorced and a single mom. The advice he gave us carried us and we still live by it today. We weren't raised to seek help, to see a counsellor or therapist. This was foreign to us. Sometimes you have to step out of your comfort zone and go down the not so familiar road to find yourself or even save yourself. Therapy in our community was a taboo, but it is such a great outlet. No person can carry everything on their shoulders without having someone to talk to. Through counselling, I was saved and my marriage too. This was a great outlet for us. It came with such great insight, realisation and tools.

Session after session, lights went on; things got better. I remember one day Rob choked me and I called Pastor Neil, and he said he wanted to see Rob immediately. He met with Rob and told him that if he ever laid his hands on me again, he would call the police himself and have him locked up. One Sunday at church, there was a call for people to come forward and be prayed for. I was very surprised when Rob got up and went to the front. He knelt down and cried like a baby. He says this was the day, the moment when the switch went on. Pastor Neil walked up to him and said, "You can cry all you want, but if you don't stop hitting Simone, God will not do anything for you." As harsh as some might think that sounds, that is exactly what Rob needed.

Rob and I have endured the rough waves, the deep valleys, and the lowest of low moments. We have struggled, we have lost so much, we have been humiliated, we were left to stand alone, we were left out in the cold, and we have gone without food to eat; not being able to feed our kids, not being able to pay school fees, and no petrol moments - even getting stuck on the side of the road with no petrol. We've even gone through abuse. Nevertheless, we pushed through. When we were given resources and the right advice, we became intentional about life. Rob started showing me that he wanted to change; he wanted to do better; he wanted to be better and I believed him. His belief made me believe. He took in all words that were shared in the sessions with Pastor Neil and used them.

Today, here we are. We have stood the test of time. I am so proud and honoured to be Mrs Robert Phillips. Not only that, I love this man simply more than he loves himself. Furthermore, I will defend and protect him, always. He is my pillar, my centre, and the poet for my warrior spirit. We all have our demons, our bad; we simply have to find that person that will help and guide us to deal with them. Robert Phillips's flaws and shortcomings were designed for me. I was built and engineered for his blueprint.

To every married couple out there; find your healthy and neural outlet because sometimes not everyone in your space is rooting for you. I realised that the voices that kept saying: "Leave him", "Divorce him", weren't for me. Be careful who you have in your inner ear, especially when it comes to your marriage and your person.

Make sure you're listening to the right voices and be sure to find your outlet to talk and open up about things. Had I listened to the voices in my inner ear, I wouldn't be where I am today. I wouldn't be experiencing the best version of Robert Phillips; the most overwhelming feeling of love. I had to silence and ignore the voices to be here today. That is the result of me not listening.

To Pastor Neil, thank you. If it wasn't for you, we would not be married today. God used you to save our marriage. Thank you for helping and guiding us. Thank you for being a healthy and neutral outlet. Thank you. May God continue to bless you for the work you do.

To Robert Phillips, thank you for sticking it out with me. Thank you for allowing me to be me; thank you for always supporting me. Thank you for fighting to be better. Thank you for opening up and dealing with your demons. Thank you for trusting me enough to share your deepest, darkest pain with remove me; thank you for becoming intentional. Thank you for rising above your past. Thank you for not allowing your past to define you. Thank you for being a present and amazing dad. Thank you for being an incredible human being.

Most importantly, thank you for becoming the man I knew you were capable of being. I will forever be by your side. You are the guy I choose to have my jungle oats, my white porridge and my Ocean Basket with.

Without you and our squad, we wouldn't have eleven years of nappies, and you wouldn't have a warrior as a partner. Thank you. I love you from my soul RD. Forever. Always. #R&S

Lessons Learnt

- Marriage is not easy, but if you have a partner who will fight with you, and for you, it makes it worth it.
- Sometimes you need to isolate yourself, your family and your marriage in order to save it.
- Finding an outlet is not a taboo; you need to talk to a neutral person.
- Don't share every problem or disagreement with family and friends because some people are secretly hoping for your downfall.
- Be very careful who you have in your inner ear. Shut out noise from family and friends.

Track 5

Father, Can You Hear Me?

Father can you hear me, we need your love today.
I know that you are listening.
You hear me every day, Father please hear us, and we will be
ok.
Father we need you to heal families today. Father can you hear
me?

SONG BY TAMELA MANN, CHERYL PEPSII RILEY, TIFFANY EVANS
& TERRELL CARTER

CHAPTER 5

Addiction & Abuse

Your Adult Drama Stems from Your Childhood Trauma.

Ever felt intense pain? Pain so intense that it literally feels as if your body is suffocating, as if your heart is being squeezed, as if your soul is pierced over and over again? Well I have. For most of my twenties this is how I felt; it was the space I was in. Let me tell you about that space.

I grew up in a bubble, so things like addiction and abuse were not terms that I knew much about. Yes I would hear about them but never bothered to delve deeply into these topics because they never affected me or someone close to me. Well, that is what I think; I could be wrong. So, getting married, I never for one second thought I would experience this, live it, see it, and feel it at such an intense level.

Between the ages of twenty and twenty-nine, I firmly believed I was married to a pathological liar. Let me break that down.

The definition of a pathological liar is: Pathological lying, also known as mythomania and pseudologia fantastica, is the chronic behaviour of compulsive or habitual lying. Unlike telling the occasional white lie to avoid hurting someone's feelings or getting in trouble, a pathological liar seems to lie for no apparent reason.

The Oxford Dictionary defines a pathological liar as a person who cannot stop telling lies. Oxford nails it. Short and to the point.

I did not understand why Rob always felt he needed to lie and he would lie about simple things, big things, random and irrelevant things. This was the reason for many of our fights and arguments. Because of my relationship with Christ, every time I would catch him out and expose him because the Holy Spirit would reveal things to me. Every day, I would cry and ask God why I was there. Little did I know all these lies needed to happen so that I would catch him out every time and confront him; he hated this. I mean, there were times when I would go to bed and wake up in the middle of the night and ask him why he gave *King's mother money without first talking to me or why he had spoken to *King's mother that day. Those incidents would plunge him into a daze and he would have that shocked look on his face. I would confront him and want answers there and then and he hated this. He hated the confrontations; he always wanted things hidden, brushed and pushed under the carpet, but the black-and-white in me left him no room for a grey playground. Confronting and exposing him were the main reasons for our physical fights and arguments. Little did I know, the roots were much deeper.

The man I married and decided to spend my life with was not only a pathological liar, but he was addicted to porn. Yes porn. It is another topic I knew absolutely nothing about. All I ever heard growing up was, sex was ugly, and it was for prostitutes and that men wanted women to be their porn stars.

That's it. I never saw or had any interest in porn, but soon, I realised that my husband was addicted to it. Again, in the early hours of the morning, I would randomly wake up and find him watching it or the Holy Spirit would tell me to check his phone and that's what I would find. Rob could never understand how I knew things; he could never grasp where my information was coming from. He would deny, deny, deny until I showed him his phone. Again, I would confront and expose him. I always thought I was not good enough for him and that is why he did the things he did, which led to me being an extremely insecure woman.

Every time I found this, I would go deeper and deeper into my shell, but little did I know; the root was much deeper.

Women. Women. Women. There always seems to be a third party involved somewhere, everywhere. Work, our social circles, everywhere I could turn. I was always left feeling embarrassed and humiliated, and again these came about through the Holy Spirit showing me things. But before things would go too far with these women, I would know. I always interrupted the beginning of his possible affairs; still I would pray that God would remove me from my marriage because I couldn't take it anymore. But He didn't. He simply kept showing me things and I would always be two steps ahead of Rob without him realising it. Even though the Holy Spirit would show me these things, it still cut deep in my soul. I was consumed by hurt; pain suffocated my very being. For the longest time, I was dealing with all this alone, no one to share with or to offload to. I was drowning in pain and my outlet was simply prayer. I was so insecure about myself and was at my lowest, and didn't like myself very much.

Furthermore, I was angry at myself because this was not the plan. This was not what I had prayed for in a partner from the age of fourteen. Not only that; I was angry, disappointed, hurt, confused, afraid, frustrated and alone. Lonely.

Little did I know, the root was much deeper.

During our period of counselling sessions with Pastor Neil, puzzle pieces started falling into place. I believe Rob realised that: "hey, this girl loves me. She is here trying to fix things", and he opened up. In 2009, having given birth to our first daughter (she was a couple of months old), we were living in his sister's garage at the time, and we were driving to an appointment. I will never forget the moment and the exact spot we were at when he said, "There is something I want to tell you." I never expected the words he uttered next, not in a million years. He was driving and looked over at me and said, "I was sexually abused by three people when I was a child." I felt as if I was kicked in the stomach. I literally lost my breath and burst into tears. I think he just wanted to get it all off his chest before the fear gripped him again. He continued, "Two of my abusers were our neighbours, a male and a female. I was six and eight when this happened, but the worst was from the age of nine years until

I was seventeen years by my uncle, *Uncle Sylvester." My heart was in so much pain. I couldn't believe what I was hearing. But he continued, "My uncle made me do things to him that are done in porn films. He would ask me to do things to him. He made me watch German porn from the age of ten and wanted me to do those things to him." Rob looked at me with tears in his eyes and continued, "I was only ten; I could never tell anyone because my Uncle Sylvester would threaten to tell my dad lies and get me into trouble. I was petrified of my dad and would just do as he said. My lying nature, my addiction to porn, my love for women and my anger stem from eight years of abuse from my uncle." He continued, "Every time you caught me out or asked me something, you were right. Every time you confronted me and wanted answers, it would make me angry and take me back to the helpless eight-year-old." Right then and there, my missing puzzle piece fell into place.

Rob lashed out all these years because he bottled up all this hurt, shame, resentment, and anger. He looked at me crying and said, "I am sorry for raising my hand to you and for hurting you." He had said this so many times prior to that day, but that day I felt him. I felt his sincerity in my soul.

Our counselling continued because now Rob had to deal with his past. He was the abused and an abuser. I had to receive counselling because I was a victim of abuse, and I was married to someone who had been abused too. We both had to learn how to deal with this matter as it was both extremely delicate and sensitive.

The day Rob opened up to both me and Pastor Neil, the shame was lifted. The devil loves secrets; he loves to keep you in that dark place. He knew if he kept Rob there, he would continue abusing me, continue watching porn and chasing every girl, but Rob decided to break that cycle. The day he opened up, everything changed. He became intentional in becoming a better man. Years of counselling allowed him to become comfortable and feel safe to open up. I am so happy that Rob found his safe place in me to share his innermost and deepest pain.

Counselling not only saved my marriage, but it saved Rob. I am incredibly proud of the journey this man has walked. He always says it was because of my love and persistence that he changed, but I refuse to take that credit. He made the conscious decision to end the cycle; he made the effort to get better.

It was a hard and painful journey, but we made it through grace.

I would never condone any kind of abuse, but this is my story and my journey. Had Rob not shown me any indication that he wanted to change after counselling, that would have meant the end of us. Counselling was my last hope.

Love Conquered.

Lessons Learnt

- Don't ever judge the next person because you have no idea what pain they may be carrying. Just because you have not experienced what they have does not make you better; it makes you human. Sprinkle them with love and grace.
- If a person doesn't think they are wrong, they will never be accountable and responsible for their actions.

Track 6

Still

Find rest my soul, in Christ alone. Know His power in
quietness and trust.
When the oceans rise and thunders roar, I will soar with you
above the storm.
Father, you are King over the flood. I will be still and know
you are God.

SONG BY HILLSONG WORSHIP

CHAPTER 6

Making Tough Decisions
Isolation, Separation & Shutting Out the Noise.

U is my Heil. U is my Toevlug. Die anker van my siel, (ek) sal U in gees en waarheid dien. U bly getrou. Die blink more ster. My liefde en lewensbron. Ek sal altyd by U wees. Daar's geen kommer en geen vrees. U is my Heil

English Translation:

You are my refuge. You are my fortress. The anchor of my soul. I will serve you in spirit & truth. You remain faithful. You are the bright morning star. My love and the source of my life. I will always be with you. There is no worry or fear. You are my refuge.

What does isolation mean?

The state of being in a place or situation that is separate from others: the condition of being isolated. The act of separating something from other things; the act of isolating something.

"U is my heil". This song carried us through our darkest and lowest moments. Listening to it today, still brings tears to my eyes because I remember where we come from, and I ask God daily to never allow me to forget where we come from. The song carried us in moments of feeling alone, worrying because we had nothing to eat, kids needing nappies, car needing petrol, and rent needed to be paid. Thank you Jesus for always providing. I am and will always be grateful.

The first ten years of Rob and I being together were about survival. Let's break down the definition of "survival"!

The definition from the Oxford Dictionary reads: Survival: the state of continuing to live or exist, often despite difficulty or danger in the struggle, battle, fight for survival.

That is exactly what we did; we survived daily. We were in survival mode; we merely existed despite the difficulty. Our marriage was in survival mode. Our parenting was in survival mode. Our finances were in survival mode. Our careers were in survival mode. We as individuals were in survival mode. We were hanging on by a thread. Grace kept us together.

We became intentional. See, sometimes it's easy to continue the cycle; to continue the washing machine effect. That is easy but when you decide to break any cycle, you need heart, time, and energy. Change does not come easily.

The mind-set had to change. Our change and becoming intentional led us to our isolation and separation period.

In this chapter, you will start to see how the wheels started turning all because we had to start making better decisions. We had to become intentional about our lives. We started by finding an outlet, which steered and guided us, and literally saved our marriage. This allowed us to start seeing our weak and trigger areas. By starting to shut out the noise, we started breaking the painful shackles.

As you know by now, we had no support, no love, and no encouragement from both sides of our families. This was very difficult, not only to understand, but also to accept. We always got the wrong advice when we asked for help. We would always hear stories about the number of children we have, our financial situation, and our struggles, but never a "Well done, you guys are managing." Outside lies and interference by family not only nearly cost us our marriage and our family, but lies from family eventually led to Rob losing *King for good. I guess that was the final nail in the coffin. But, it is never over until God decides it is.

Our counselling sessions brought us to a point where we realised that both sides of our families were no good for us as individuals, our marriage, and our children. We had to take some hard decisions. After ten years of back-and-forth, looking for love and acceptance from families, we had to decide what was best for us. Our families were no good for us and had we continued expecting help from them, our marriage would not have survived. We needed to build up our foundation; yes; ten years in, we didn't have one, but it wasn't too late. We had to build up our strength as individuals, as a married couple, and as a family because we didn't have our own strength, our own voice, and our own identity. We were too needy and reliant on others who were family.

Counselling allowed us to deal with ourselves as individuals and as a married couple and it opened wounds, allowing for healing and clarity. We couldn't see what was being done to us because we were so lost. We were bleeding with pain, so the water always seemed murky. But counselling allowed for the waters to become clear and we could start seeing things clearly.

One day, I said to Rob, "I am done." He looked at me and asked, "With?"

I explained that I was done with families. Not only that, but I would no longer be visiting any family. I refused to sit around people who belittled him, who disrespected him and had no regard for our marriage or our children. What kind of parent and wife would I be if I sat in the company of people who disrespected my husband and the father of my children?

I cannot and will not give anyone permission to belittle and disregard the father of my children; not in my presence, and definitely not in the presence of my children. No one has the right to change the perception our children have of their father. He is the only person who would change their perception about him.

I said to him he is welcome to visit if he wished, but the children and I would not. He looked at me and said, "We are in this together." And that was it. We isolated ourselves for three full years and we realised it was the best decision we made; it saved us. With no outside noise, we found each other. We rekindled the love we had, but on another level. We reconnected with our children. It was us against the world. The minute we shut families out, favour started to find us all round. That is where the intense love and protective warrior was born. She started to find her roar.

Bonus Track

Roar

I used to bite my tongue and hold my breath.
Scared to rock the boat and make a mess so I sat quietly,
agreed politely I guess that I forgot I had a choice. I let you
push me past the breaking point. I stood for nothing, so I fell
for everything.
You held me down, but I got up (hey) already brushing off the
dust. You hear my voice, you hear that sound. Like thunder,
gonna shake the ground. You held me down, but I got up (hey)
Get ready 'cause I've had enough. I see it all, I see it now I got
the eye of the tiger, a fighter dancing through the fire 'cause I
am a champion, and you're gonna hear me roar. Louder,
louder than a lion 'cause I am a champion, and you're going to
hear me roar.

SONG BY KATY PERRY

Lessons Learnt

- Sometimes in your marriage and in life, you need to make hard decisions that not everyone will like or appreciate, but are best for you and your family.
- Isolation is the mechanism I used to protect my family, and it has worked for us. It has taught me that I need to protect my husband and children no matter what.

Track 7

Money On My Mind

When I go home
I tend to close the door
I never wanted more
So sing with me
Can't you see
I don't have
Money on my mind
Money on my mind
I do it for
I do it for the love

SONG BY SAM SMITH

CHAPTER 7

Finances, Money, Currency, Cash

Such an important yet sensitive topic within marriage. How can you have clarity about money when you have no clarity about yourself and your life?

For the first ten years, our marriage was not stable and neither were our lives, which caused us to lose so much and we made many bad financial decisions simply because we weren't operating from a place of clarity, a place of unity, or from a place of love. Back then I had no clue about Rob's salary. All I knew was what he had to do. Whether he could or couldn't was never my concern. I made sure that I performed my financial responsibilities too and that was it. We never sat with our monthly salaries, never worked out a budget and that is simply because we had no clarity and no direction. We were just flowing month to month, hoping to make it. In hindsight, the first ten years taught me that our finances are a reflection of our minds.

How can you be clear on your money when you aren't clear about yourself?

Let me share the following situations which were painful points for me and defining moments:

1. 15th June 2009, the coldest day of that year; I will never forget that day. Rob and I were both not working and had to make plans to move, but in the interim our electricity was disconnected. Our daughter was a month old, and it was below freezing. My in-laws were down the road, but we couldn't go to them. Rob and I slept on the floor and we had the kids sleep on the bed.

We eventually moved in with my mother, which was a bad decision. My own mother ill-treated us (including our kids); she would buy things and hide them from our kids. She wouldn't cook for us, so we had to see to ourselves. When Rob got a job, he would get up at 4:30am every morning to catch the 5:30am bus, and he would be back by 6:30pm. He would leave when it was dark and come home when it was dark. His salary was meagre; not much at all, but he worked hard and became number one. After a brief stint, he was offered a better job and package. Every day I would be on my knees praying for a breakthrough, asking God to open a door so that we could get our own place. One day while I was on maternity leave, a lump sum of my maternity benefit (UIF) came through and it was enough to deposit our own place and pay rent for one month.

2. In June 2010, when the world and South Africa were in full celebration mood for the World Cup, I was job hunting. I needed a job and I was called for an interview in Sandton, Johannesburg. It was one of Africa's leading financial services organisations, which provides retirements, asset management and insurance, and wealth management solutions. My interview went so well I was convinced the job was mine; just to get a call saying my interview went really well, however, they couldn't hire me because "someone" had called the human resources department and told them not to hire me because I was a bad mother and I was abusing my stepson. How could your own family do that to you? If I was not working, it meant my children would suffer. Why would anyone want my children to suffer? Why?

3. In August 2011, I finally started a new job. I was beyond relieved and happy. On the day I got the news that I got the job, I was sitting in the middle of Johannesburg central having my hair braided, and I was listening to music when my phone rang. It was the general manager letting me know that I had been successful and that I got the job. Having been unemployed for over a year, I sat in the middle of the city centre and started to cry right there. The ladies who were busy with my hair started to panic wondering what was wrong, and I looked at them and said, "God just remembered me." I sobbed non-stop and continued listening to my music. The song that played was Israel Houghton's "Alpha and Omega", and I associate the song with that moment in my life. I sat there and all that could come from my lips was: "Thank you, Jesus." These lyrics will always be with me:

> You are Alpha and Omega
> we worship you our Lord,

you are worthy to be praised
We give you all the glory,
we worship, you our Lord,
You are worthy to be praised
We give You all the glory,
(And we worship You)
We worship You our Lord
You are worthy to be praised

4. In August 2012 we went from earning two salaries to one for nine months; the hardest time of our lives. Rob was unemployed for nine months. My salary would literally pay our rent and that was it. We couldn't even squeeze in our bills, food, and petrol. However, during those nine months, Robert Phillips experienced a rebirth. He reconnected with God on another level. I have never seen my husband so low, but at the same time so close to God and so sincere. In those nine months, God needed to isolate and deal with the head of our home. During those nine months, I prayed for Rob more than I did for myself. At the time, our kids' ages were: seven, five, three and the youngest was a couple of months old and Rob was at home with them. The boys were in school, and so he would get them ready in the mornings and pick them up in the afternoon. Deciding to live in the place we were renting at the time was probably one of the worst decisions we have ever made for our family. We had a landlord who simply did not care. One Sunday evening, he came to the house with a group of men who started breaking down the doors and attacking us, while the kids were inside the house. We got out of the house, and drove straight to the police station, but we were unfortunate because we were sent from one station to the other; no one wanted to help. We later found out that they were all in the landlord's pockets.

That evening we had to call my sister for a place to stay because we couldn't continue staying there. We drove at midnight to her place, not realising that we were going from one hellhole to another. Our kids were so traumatised, they didn't sleep for nights on end. Rob and I slept on the floor so that the kids could sleep comfortably. The very next morning, Rob was offered two job opportunities with two great packages. Now look at God? From being unemployed to being able to choose, but he had to learn the lesson so that he could be grateful for his job and for him to know who his maker is.

Looking back, it's as if the place we were living in was a hole we couldn't get out of and that we had to be violently removed for our breakthrough to come, but at that moment, it was so hard. It is one of the toughest times we have had to face as a family. God had to literally remove us from this environment for a breakthrough to come. Sometimes the environment you are in is holding you back; it is hindering your blessing. The incident left us with some emotional scars and to this day, I still cry when I think, talk, or even write about it. So Rob picked the job that would work out best for us and both of us were working, finally. We were still living with my sister during this time, and the kids would be home with certain family members. One day; I will never forget my kids' faces on that day for as long as I live; when we walked in, my kids were sitting on the stairs with tears in their eyes. They cried when they saw Rob and I. When we asked what had happened, our son said they were not allowed to watch TV, couldn't play, and had to wait for me to get home for them to eat. Now, we had sold most of the big furniture items, but took some of our stuff to my sister's place. The items included our DSTV decoder and we made sure there was food, especially things the kids enjoyed. I was hurt that my own flesh and blood treated my kids so bad.

Our kids had just experienced a very traumatic event and here we had people adding to their emotional scars. I was not happy and as a result we were kicked out. Yes we were told to leave with our kids; a month later, we had to leave. Rob's first salary after nine months paid the deposit and rental for a new place to stay. We could only afford a two-bedroom place. We moved in with no couches and a few other things, but we made it work. We were together, we lived, we laughed, and we loved. In that time, I lost my hair; I had to shave my head. Little did I know that was my rebirth. In that small place we started building toward our next. We were on our own and we had to trust strangers to take care of our kids because it was just us. We had to send our kids for therapy, especially our eldest.

One Sunday we were at church and we had a guest speaker from Cape Town, Pastor Ross. The title of his sermon was: "Your Miracle" and to this day the sermon still speaks to Rob. Rob always remembers the line: "Your miracle will only come if you make the right decisions." Right there, the change happened for us financially. Just that line.

We realised money was not the problem; money was always there. It was our decision-making that was the problem and our decision-making changed. And trust me when I say our financial situation changed; it really did. Money was still the same, but better decisions allowed us to live a more comfortable life. See, when your relationship is unstable and your mind is not clear, the instability will first reflect in your finances.

Today, we know what each of us earns; we work out a budget together monthly, and have cards and access to each other's bank accounts. We both are on the same page at all times because we both now have clear minds about what we want and we share a vision for our family and our future. Everything is so clear and transparent now that if one is unable to meet one or two of their responsibilities, the other is aware and helps out. We are now able to support and carry each other. That is what partners do. That doesn't make either one of us weak, because we are partners striving towards the same goal. We can now make the load lighter for each other because the lines of communication are clear and open.

Before this turnaround, if I asked Rob for something, he would say: "No", I would be angry for days and take great offence to that "No". I would even go as far as saying that he never wanted to do anything for me, so he did not love me. But today if he says "No", I don't even get upset. Why? Because I know Rob loves me with his being and if he says "No" it's not because he is being malicious; it is because he simply cannot do it at that particular moment. And today I respect his "No". I am testament of this statement: Your finances speak to your mindset.

As Tony Robbins says: "Energy flows where attention goes. To get what you really want in life, you need a clear goal that has purpose and meaning behind it. Once this is in place, you can focus your energy on the goal and become obsessive about it. When you learn how to focus your energy, amazing things happen."

A stable relationship often involves planning a future; whatever that looks like... renting together, buying a house, owning cars, having kids, and taking lots of holidays. Whatever your path looks like, money is important, because where you spend it dictates how you live and how you achieve your goals together.

Lessons Learnt

• Don't discuss too much of you with people, including family. I was completely broken because our household continued to limp on with one salary.

• God will literally remove you from an environment in order for your blessing to come. Sometimes it is the environment that is holding you back. Too much noise does not allow for your energy to flow in the right direction.

• Play everything close to your chest. Not everyone needs to know everything about you.

• People, including family, do not want you to succeed. We figured that certain family members would prefer us living on the street or in a shelter with nothing, living with our hands out and being at their mercy. I refuse to be at the mercy of a human being.

Track 8

Can't Give Up Now

There will be mountains that I will have to climb. And there
will be battles
that I will have to fight, but victory or defeat it's up to me to
decide. But how can I expect to win if I never try, I just can't
give up now. I've come too far from where I started from,
nobody told me the road would be easy, and I don't believe
He's brought me this far to leave me.

SONG BY MARY MARY

CHAPTER 8

Existing, Not Living

An insecure person lacks confidence in their own value and one or more of their capabilities. The person lacks trust in themselves or others, and has ever-lingering fear that the present positive state is temporary and would let them down by "going wrong" in the future.

What causes insecurity?

Most of us feel insecure sometimes, but some of us feel this most of the time. The kind of childhood you had, past traumas, recent experiences of failure or rejection, loneliness, social anxiety, negative beliefs about yourself, perfectionism, or having a critical parent or partner, can all contribute to insecurity.

From the age of twenty to the age of twenty-nine, I merely existed. I did not live. I was completely lost, forgot myself and was insecure. I didn't know who I was or even understand myself. Not only that, but I was coasting along and only wearing my wife and mom cap; I did not even wear the woman cap. Furthermore, I was at my lowest and a complete emotional wreck.

Stepping into my husband's family, I was young and still looking for my path. Little did I know that finding my path would take me ten years, the hardest ten years of my existence. Up until the age of nineteen, I thought I loved myself and looked after myself. I thought I was strong enough but man, my foundation was shaken and turned completely upside-down.

From 2004 up until 2014, I had a rude awakening. During this period, my insecurity level was at its peak. I guess I was always made to feel I wasn't good enough and at some point, I started believing this narrative that others peddled about me. I started thinking the labels placed on me were true. My complexion was a subject that always seemed to come up in conversations, because I was not fair enough and my hair not straight enough. However, as much as it affected me on the surface, my soul couldn't accept these. My mind and soul were always at war.

I can admit I started to not like myself very much, let alone love myself. Lack of self-love can stem from growing up in a family where love is conditional, being in a relationship where you weren't or aren't valued, or a number of other triggers. I lost complete faith in myself. I lost my value and my worth. If you had to ask me during that period who Semonia Maureen was or what she liked, I wouldn't have been able to answer you, purely because I myself did not know. My struggles ran deep.

Having had four kids within a space of eight years took a massive toll on me, not only physically but emotionally. After the birth of our second son in 2007, I gained eighteen kilograms and battled to shed the weight. Battled. This threw any bit of confidence I may have had right out of the window. My weight and body changes made me insecure and conscious about myself and my shortcomings. I was in a deep dark pit of insecurity and uncertainty. I would look at myself in the mirror and cry and I did not like myself. Not only that, I saw a heavy me, with cellulite and not so perky boobs. Likewise, I saw a little girl who was lost, ashamed, angry, and alone.

Every day, I would put on my best for work and the smile everyone always complimented me on, but deep down the pain ran deep. The uncertainty, the worthlessness, and aloneness were exploding on the inside. I had my battles I had to fight every morning when I woke up and every evening when I came from work. I had to deal with me. I spent my days crying, went to bed crying, and woke up crying. I did this for a long time.

I did not want to be around people. Invites would come, but I simply would not want to attend. I wanted to hide, thinking that would heal me or make me better and I hoped no one would see the lost and broken me. One sign of insecurity is low self-esteem or negative self-image, particularly when your image seems to be inconsistent with outside narratives and labels. Low self-esteem means you think badly about yourself or your abilities, which was definitely me. Eventually, it led to other problems, especially concerning mental health.

My struggles with myself ran deep. I had such low esteem that I guess it made it easier for Rob to lie to me and abuse me. The abuse made me go deeper into the pit, the narrative of not being good enough would pop up often. It was at the back of my mind. I would ask myself: Is he abusing me and treating me so bad because I am not good enough? Again the mind and soul battle continued.

My mental health was non-existent; I didn't even know about mental health. I could say I was depressed for a period, but never labelled it, because I didn't understand it. Before we got our counselling or therapy outlet, prayer was all I had. It was all I could do. I cried so much in my twenties; today when I do cry, you must understand that my heart strings have been touched or my soul is pierced.

Insecurity in a woman can sometimes be hard to spot — or worse, sometimes you think it's ok. A person who is dating or married to an insecure person will definitely feel as if they have the upper hand in a relationship and that was Rob. Insecurity is the root of a lot of issues in relationships. You've undoubtedly heard it before that solid relationships are built on trust, or at least something to that effect, and I think most people would find it difficult to dispute this.

The following are twelve signs of insecurity which I experienced:

1. I didn't believe I was enough.

I was sensitive to criticism and my feelings were hurt easily. Sometimes, I was not sure if I even deserved to be in a good relationship or have a great career or be paid my worth.

2. I had a difficult time saying "no" and I had no boundaries.
Not only did I want others to be happy, but I also wanted to be agreeable. I showed up to help others. I'd go out of my way to be there for others, and I was present for the people I cared about.

3. I felt I had to please others.
Because I was not rooted in my own worth, I would go out of my way to make others happy. A lack of inner love translates into a need for constant approval and appreciation by others and that was me.

4. I compared myself to others every chance I got.
I always felt the urge to compare myself to others. I would go out of my way to look for people who were smarter, kinder, better-looking, healthier, nicer, friendlier, etc.

5. I didn't believe I could do anything right.
I focused on my mistakes, faults, flaws and inadequacies. I imagined the worst-case scenario in every situation and expected that I would mess up.

6. I was self-conscious of my body.
I didn't like looking in the mirror and I always found ways to have negative self-talk when thinking about my body.

7. I felt ashamed of myself.
I was embarrassed often and just wanted to hide myself or fade into the background of social situations.

8. I couldn't take a compliment.

People who are insecure usually don't deal very well with compliments. That was me. I would brush it off. I felt as though I was unworthy of what people were saying about me.

9. I put myself down.
Because I was insecure in my mind, I couldn't do anything right and therefore I put myself down. There is a fine line between modesty and being cruel to yourself.

10. I hid parts of me.
I found myself constantly trying to hide things and conceal truths from the people in my life.

11. I accepted less than I deserved.
I didn't think much of myself. So if you find yourself constantly running back to people who aren't good to you or allowing people to walk all over you, the problem might be more than just your huge heart or your tendency to see the best in people. It might mean you don't have much respect for yourself and that's a shame because you totally deserve to be respected. You don't have to be completely ruthless with people, but you do have to demand respect by respecting yourself first.

12. I put up a front.
I allowed people to see what I wanted them to see: the surface. If you're obsessed with creating a perfect image of yourself for other people to comment on, then you're uncomfortable with the real you. Not only are there different types of insecurity, but there also different causes or triggers of insecurities.

Below is some content from *On Everyone's Lips* podcast.

1. Traumatic Events.

Any event that causes serious physical, emotional, or psychological damage is considered traumatic. Examples of traumatic events include being involved in a serious road accident, rape, or even losing a loved one. If proper measures are not taken on time, these events may leave the victims with long-term consequences like rapid feelings of fear, which manifest in the form of social insecurity.

2. Low Self-Esteem.

Characterised by a negative feeling about oneself as well as the lack of confidence, low self-esteem can make you feel as though people hate you and do not want to associate with you (social and personal insecurity). Low self-esteem can also affect your work since it makes you feel incompetent, hence makes you afraid of losing your job or business (professional insecurity).

3. Body Image.

The way you perceive your body affects how you feel about yourself. If you think your body is not attractive, you will feel bad about yourself. For instance, you may regard your body as overweight or underweight and hence not attractive enough. This also relates to the way you compare your body to those of other people, especially celebrities. This is greatly related to social and personal insecurities.

4. Violence.

If you are a victim of any form of violence, you are likely to develop a form of insecurity. For example, if you are a victim of attempted molestation or rape, you may end up feeling uncomfortable around strangers of the opposite sex. Also, your trust in people diminishes, making it difficult for you to form new relationships.

5. Abuse.

Being abused involves being treated with cruelty, that is, physically, emotionally, financially, sexually, or culturally; for instance, being a victim of domestic abuse (physical abuse). Financial abuse happens when a partner controls all the household budgeting or when one opens a credit account using the other person's details without their knowledge.

6. Comparing Yourself to Others.

You can perceive yourself as not good enough when you compare yourself to others. For instance, you may compare yourself with others in terms of looks, education level, or the kind of job they have, among other factors. Comparing yourself to others can make you feel awkward and consequently, unable to interact properly with others.

7. Fear and failure.

You may be afraid of something, or someone. Even though fear is normal, fear becomes a problem when it takes over your life. It may even affect how you do your job as well as how you interact with others. Fear may result from failing at something.

Lessons Learnt

- I need to love and accept myself before I can ask Rob to.
- Everything starts with me.
- Love yourself unconditionally and fearlessly.

Corporate

Track 9

No Longer A Slave

I'm no longer a slave to fear. I am a child of God. I'm no longer a slave to fear. I am a child of God. From my mother's womb. You have chosen me.
Love has called my name, I've been born again to a family.
Your blood flows through my veins. I'm no longer a slave to fear, I am a child of God. I'm no longer a slave to fear, I am a child of God, and I'm no longer a slave to fear. I am a child of God
I'm no longer a slave to fear. I am a child of God

SONG BY BETHEL MUSIC

CHAPTER 9

15 Years A Slave

I matriculated in 2001 and with everything in me, I wanted to study travel and tourism, but financially that was not viable. So instead, I went for a computer course to become computer-literate and joined a recruitment agency because the next best thing for me to do was to find a job.

And then began corporate life. I was so excited to be working and earning a salary; little did I know where the journey would go.

March 2003, I started working at one of the top four banks in South Africa as a temp; I was an adult, so I thought. The working life required discipline and punctuality, so I had to adapt quickly. Soon the contract ended, and I moved to another temporary assignment at another of the top four banks. The contract lasted only six months. I started observing and got a feel of corporate life; or so I thought. Little did I know my bubble would be popped.

In March 2004, I started working at one of the biggest financial services companies within the short-term insurance space. My journey as a permanent employee began, very different from that as a temp employee. This is where I started to see favouritism, nepotism, and racism at its peak, and most people did not confront these vices; they turned the other cheek because they valued their salaries. I was never one not to speak up and voice my opinion.

I had my first clash with my line manager, who was white, in 2004. The source of our conflict was the discrimination I saw there. I felt non-Whites were treated differently in terms of working hours, leave etc. as opposed to my white colleagues and I brought it to his attention. As young as I was, at the age of twenty-one, I saw the wrath of white corporate. It was a complete shock for me. I was eventually moved to another department because my voice became too loud. I eventually decided to leave the company two years later. I realised that my little voice was not going to change something that most people were so comfortable with. My moral compass wouldn't let me stay, not even for a salary. My black-and-white side started showing up more strongly.

In June 2006, I started my new employment with confidence because of the qualifications and experience I had gained from the previous company. I worked in one department (which I absolutely loved) for nine months and my team leader recommended me for a position at head office. I applied and got the job. It was something different and new, and I enjoyed the work. Again, I landed in a department where the majority of my colleagues were white and had more privileges than other ethnic groups.

I fell pregnant and went on maternity leave. I was due back on 1 December, but it was unfortunate that our second born was a breast-only baby and only wanted me; no one could babysit him, not even Rob. We tried nursery school, a day mom, a full time helper, nothing worked. I called my line manager to ask if I could take unpaid leave until the 15th of December because Rob would be on leave thereafter and he would stay home with the baby. Without thinking twice, she showed no empathy towards me or my situation and declined my request; she said I had better be back in the office on 1 December. I spoke to Rob and we decided it would be best for me to resign until our son was ok, and that is what I did. She did not even respond to my resignation email; I got a response from HR. The same demon followed me, but I simply left.

After nine months, I went back into the market, got a job at a small brokerage, worked there for a few months until I decided to keep my options open for a better opportunity, and it came. In December 2008, I got a permanent job at one of the biggest brokerages at the time; I enjoyed my job and what I did. I had a structure to my duties and knew exactly what was required of me. Rob started working at the same company but a different department, and he had an incident with my line manager which involved one of my colleagues and one of his; we considered both of them our friends. Both these "friends" were asked to lie and fabricate lies about the incident that happened and they obliged. I was shocked to my core at the lengths people would go to save themselves and their jobs. Again the moral compass was not having it and I moved on, but soon after my departure, the entire company was sold and most people were retrenched.

Between 2009 and 2014, I worked for two smaller companies. I absolutely loved one of these companies because I enjoyed my job; I was good at it and I got along with my boss and had nothing to complain about. I thought bigger was bigger. Big mistake.

Piece of advice; bigger is not always better. Sometimes the big beautiful building you see on the outside is just smoke and mirrors and is actually a complete hellhole on the inside. Think carefully.

Another big company made me an offer and I didn't hesitate after seeing the package and the benefits. The smaller company was willing to counter-offer and promote me, but stupid naïve me thought the big company would be best, probably one of my biggest mistakes, but God knew why I had to embark on this journey. In February 2014, I started at the big internationally recognised company, and I was so happy. Short-lived. I have always been a hard worker and always put my best foot forward and this started being noticed. I was given more responsibilities and left in charge when management was not around. Not only that, I even got to handle high net worth client queries and complaints.

Likewise, I had colleagues I considered friends. Furthermore, I thought I had a good working relationship with my line manager. At some point, the company was planning to acquire another book of business and my line manager called me in and told me she wanted to promote me to team leader once the merger happened, but soon cracks started showing, and things changed when I started to question things.

We had a team assistant who had no experience in what we did, but because her mother was the PA to the CEO, she got the job and had many liberties. She had no set working hours, took leave when she wanted, half the time did not even complete leave forms etc. At one point, my leave was approved then later declined because she suddenly needed to take leave for a family holiday.

I took the matter to HR, but it was as if the HR dreaded my line manager because of her good relationship with the CEO. I realised that it was not about the company's code of conduct or ethics and values, but about whom you knew. The HR was too scared to reprimand my line manager, she would agree with me in our meetings but sing a completely different song when my line manager was around. I would always call her out on it. Nevertheless, I still worked and gave my best.

Furthermore, I had made a friend, *Kathy, at one of the companies I worked for and she was supporting her family and really needed a better salary and benefits, so I put in a good word for her with my line manager and vouched for her work ethic, and she got the job. Once she got the job, she completely changed, she started causing problems for me at work, saying I did not do certain things, complaining about me and spreading all sorts of lies and even went as far as having an investigation launched against me. *Kathy made me see her for who she truly was. I thought I was helping her out, but she also showed me that my line manager wanted her team members to backstab each other by carrying stories to her and enjoyed the friction within the team.

Again, I saw people for who they really are. *Kathy showed me flames, I thought we were "friends" but actually we were far from it; we were complete strangers. I came to realise that *Kathy actually wanted my seat even if it meant lying. She did it, not realising how hard I had worked to be where I was. She wormed her way into my line manager's good books at my expense and made life very hard for me. I was in the HR officer's office every other day. My manager started looking for faults so that she could get rid of me. She declined my leave and her reasons were never valid but seemed to make "business sense" to the HR; a phrase I heard so often.

The egoistical, arrogant, white privilege demon and the fake friends lesson I still did not learn and had not overcome came my way again, and it became too much for me, so yes, I resigned.

I still did not get that I needed to be taught something. I had all these red flags waving right in front of my face, some knocking me in the face, but I was hell-bent on being in corporate. I believed I had to work; my family needed me to work. Not only that, but I had no choice. Furthermore, I believed I was a good employee. I worked hard, always gave my best, never had a warning to my name or put through a disciplinary hearing and I always succeeded in my roles, but I was not happy. My job did not make me happy. Corporate took bits of my soul every day; I only did it because I had to.

Track 10

What A Beautiful Name

You were the Word at the beginning, one with God the Lord
Most High. Your hidden glory in Creation. Now revealed in
You our Christ. Death could not hold You. The veil tore before
You, You silenced the boast of sin and grave. The heavens are
roaring, the praise of Your glory. For You are raised to life
again.
You have no rival. You have no equal
now and forever, God You reign, yours is the kingdom.
Yours is the glory, Yours is the Name above all names.

SONG BY HILLSONG WORSHIP

CHAPTER 10

Termination Notice Served

In 2017, it was time to step into the corporate ring one last time and stand until the last round with a TKO in hand.

Another big company, beautiful building, and manicured lawns is where it all ended for me, but this involved heads of departments, the CEO himself, appointing an attorney, and me heading to the CCMA. I was built for this round; see all those times I simply walked away and moved on, but not this time.

I started at this company in March 2017, little did I know that I would be seconded to another company whose MD clearly disliked non-whites, had her daughter as a manager, but with no experience or qualifications, and her son-in-law as the IT manager, and my manager who had no experience in what we did. Already I knew that we would experience problems. As time passed, I started observing things and seeing red flags and this time I made sure I paid attention.

Red Flag 1:
White staff were at the office at 7:00am, supposed to be working, but they would be outside on the balcony smoking and chatting until 8:30am. If clients called during this time, we were told to tell them that the staff were in meetings or unavailable.

Red Flag 2:
Every day between 14:30pm and 15:30pm all the white staff would get up and leave. All non-white staff worked until 5pm, non-negotiable.

Red Flag 3:
Non-white staff's leave was dependent on a white staff member. I remember my leave was approved and two weeks before my leave, I was called in just to be told my leave had been declined because one of my white colleagues needed to go on holiday abroad with his wife. Another time I was told I couldn't leave early to take my kid to the doctors because my white colleague's dog needed to be vaccinated.

Red Flag 4:
This company had nepotism on another level; family did not have to complete leave forms, yet every week for at least two to three days family members were not in the office. Now, I observed this and still continued to work, again giving my best. No one could ever fault me when it came to my work. I never wanted to give people a reason to talk about me, especially when it came to my work. I kept my nose clean. But that didn't stop the tornado that was about to hit.

June 2017: The tornado began.

We worked in a call centre and were never relieved or assisted by other departments or the non-white staff; we would skip breaks because we would have call after call. As a result, I got a bladder infection because I couldn't relieve myself when I needed to. I went to see the doctor on this day because I was in excruciating pain. I was booked off on the 16th and 17th of November. Immediately, I notified my manager (the son-in-law of the director) and sent him a copy of my doctor's note. In my opinion, I had followed the process.

Well, not according to the daughter, who had no business with me. She decided not to call me, but to call Rob to ask him where I was. Rob responded that I did notify my manager and that I had been booked off with a sick note. She then asked him, "So when does she want to come back?" Obviously Rob let me know and I immediately emailed my manager to ask what the problem was because I had notified him. This email had the MD so mad. Who did I think I was to question her daughter? I asked her the same: who did her daughter think she was questioning my husband about me? I told the MD that I had no business with her daughter.

I shouldn't have said that because HR (Human Resources), another weak, young and naïve HR consultant, was called and we had a meeting. She couldn't mediate the meeting and was bullied by the MD. From that meeting my reporting line was changed and guess what? The MD, her daughter, and her son started building a case against me.

I started to voice the unfair treatment towards non-white staff and suddenly our working hours changed. I spoke about every unfair practise that took place. Furthermore, this is when I started to experience corporate cover up at a level I never experienced in the fifteen years of my working experience. From lies, coercing, colluding, backstabbing and forgery; it all happened to me.

September 2017 everything exploded. The MD made my life a living hell and the HR officer was all for the MD, too scared to tell her she was wrong.

I couldn't handle the discrimination and victimisation any longer. As an employee, I was entitled to follow procedures and seeing that the HR completely failed to fulfil her role as a neutral person, I was left no choice. I had endless meetings with different HR officers, who according to me were too weak and too scared of the MD who thought she was my Jesus. She thought she was my beginning and my end. Little did she know, I serve the Alpha and Omega. I remember she once said to me in front of the weak and scared HR consultant, "Many of your people tried to take me on, none got it right and neither will you. No one can and will ever touch me." I got up and said, "Watch me, remember these words, touch not my anointed", and left her office. Little did she and I both know that God, the Alpha and Omega's hand was in what was about to transpire.

In September, I lodged a grievance. Now most corporate companies have all these wonderful policies and procedures in place, but I learnt these are not there to help and assist the employee, no ways. Man did I have to learn?

Below are definitions of a grievance:

1. A real or imagined cause for complaint, especially unfair treatment.

2. An official statement of a complaint over something believed to be wrong or unfair.

3. A feeling of resentment over something believed to be wrong or unfair.

That explains why I followed the procedure just to be shot down with many different reasons. To top it off, I was advised to take a mutual separation. What a joke! The MD and her wrongs were not addressed, not at all. She won Round One.

Let's define mutual separation: A Mutual Separation Agreement is effectively an agreement between the employer and employee setting out the terms and conditions of an employee's termination of employment. In ideal circumstances, both parties are happy with the contents of these agreements, but this is not always the case.

When I was offered one, I asked a simple question: "Who benefits from this?" Definitely not me and my family, so it's not going to happen. I declined the offer. Then the next offer came, to "try" to find me a position within the company. I sent my resume to the HR person, and might I add at the time many posts that needed my skills and knowledge were available, but guess what? Suddenly, I was not "experienced" for the posts. Game recognised game. They wanted me to stay and make my life a living hell to a point where I would be left with no choice but to leave because of the circumstances. Little did they know, the Alpha and Omega was at work.

I stayed at the company and worked, but kept my nose clean. I was still treated unfairly and victimised constantly. I would let the "new" HR assigned to me know of what was going on each and every time, not realising that I was creating a paper trail.

9 October 2017, I was called to a meeting with HR, the MD, and the head of HR to be told I was suspended. When I asked what for, I was told it was about a client complaint, which I was never asked about and was not aware of, but the MD said the charge sheet would provide the details. I knew the MD, her son-in-law, her daughter, and my so-called "colleagues" were up to something because they were too quiet, and in and out of meetings, and one could feel the tension in the room. People literally stopped speaking to me. In my suspension, the company did not even follow its own suspension policy, I brought this to their attention, but nothing was done. Again, I did not notice the paper trial I was creating.

17 October 2017, I received my charge sheet and a bundle of evidence and guess what? I had seven charges against me, yes seven; some dating back to May 2017. None of the chargers were ever discussed with me. I was suspended and charged by the company I was seconded to, but which was not my employer. Interestingly, I was issued with a final written warning by my employer; like how crazy is that? I am no law degree graduate, but I do have logic and everything about my entire process was not in line with the labour laws of our country, so Rob and I decided to appoint a lawyer to help defend me in the charges I was facing. He was extremely helpful, and we went through

every charge carefully and prepared a defence against each charge, with the law and the correct evidence backing it up.

We came across a form where my signature was forged by the MD's son-in-law. I reported this to the SAPS, to the company's internal forensic team, and to the head of HR and the CEO. Yes my case drew the attention of the heads of the company, including the CEO; they would all sit in meetings discussing it. Again, I was not realising that I was creating a paper trail.

My lawyer and I often met and talked even more telephonically, because any time I felt unsure or confused, I would message or call to get clarity, and he never hesitated to help. He knew about the company and how it operated, and it did not have a good reputation out in the public when it came to how it treated its staff. He once told me, the company had a savings account for matters that were taken to the Commission for Conciliation, Mediation and Arbitration (CCMA), so I had to brace myself.

The CCMA is an independent body (not linked to any political party, union or business) that aims to promote fair labour practices by resolving labour disputes between employees and employers.

During this time, we were living in a secure complex, so we knew most of the people and most knew us. While I was preparing for my hearing, one day we heard a knock on our door, Rob opened and it was one of our neighbours who loved playing soccer with our boys. He told Rob that while he was on his way to the shop that day he was stopped outside the complex by a white guy who was driving a white car. The guy had a picture in his hand and he had asked if he knew the lady in the picture and if she stayed in the complex.

When he looked at the picture, he noticed it was me and my children. At that moment the Holy Spirit said I must show him the picture on the fridge, which I did. I showed him the picture, and he said that's the picture he had seen earlier in the day. He continued to say he asked the guy why he was looking for me and he blurted out that he was investigating me for insurance fraud. The minute I heard that, I knew that the MD had sent this man to my home with the same picture I had on my desktop at the time.

She took an image of the picture using her phone because our neighbour said the picture was on this man's phone. The MD went as far as stalking me! Rob and I went to the security guard at the gate to ask if someone had been there that day asking about me, and his response was that no one had. The CCTV footage didn't show anyone either, which meant he knew the property had cameras. I reported this incident to the SAPS and to the company, my "employer". I made it clear that if anything happened to me or my family, this is the person they needed to find.

Right after raising a few concerns with my employer, the MD of the seconded company got her lawyer friend to email me, to basically threaten me. I sent this very email to the HR team, executives, and the CEO himself and told them that I was tired of this woman and that I would not be backing down. Now, normally by now I would have resigned.

During my suspension, I cried a lot; I could hardly sleep. I was anxious all the time. For the first time in my life I had to be on calming and sleeping tablets; that's how bad it became. I was in hell for a good couple of months.

On the day of my hearing, it was clear the chairperson could tell I had assistance from a legal brain. My colleagues came to the hearing and sat across me at the table and lied about me, just to keep their jobs. I mean these are people I would pray with, talk with, have lunch with, encourage and even help at times. I mean, there was one I had known for many years. We had started working together in 2004; she was even at my wedding, yet she lied. She typed a long email telling all sorts of lies about me, complaining about me, just to save her job; the very job I helped her get because I got in touch with her when it became available. I knew she had three boys and was a single mom, so I got her resume and vouched for her 100%, yes another "friend" that I thought I was helping came and caused havoc. Because she wanted my chair; she betrayed me. Still I had not learnt my lesson but look at God.

I used these so-called friends' WhatsApp messages to me against them in the meeting; I also had to defend myself because no one was willing to. They were all too scared to lose their jobs, so the mantra was: money over the truth and money over integrity. I was alone besides Rob and our lawyer. I defended myself and was found not guilty.

I went back to work, had a new line manager, another one who was weak and scared of the "MD", not realising the "MD" became an employer just like the rest of us. There was no longer a seconding company; everyone reported to my employer. We non-whites had more flexible working hours and people were treated with some dignity. I saw slight changes.

Then it happened. January 2018 came. I had applied for leave in October 2017 for January 2018 because I would always take leave on the first week of schools' re-opening. This leave was already approved in October, but I was once again told that my leave was yet again declined so that one of my white colleagues could take hers; it was a leave that she had just applied for. I was not having it. I went to my new line manager and told her that my leave had been approved and I would be taking it.

Guess what, I was suspended again; this time for one charge - gross insubordination. My lawyer already said to me that I needed to prepare myself for a dismissal. The company wanted to get rid of me, which was hard because I was not a bad or ill-disciplined employee. I just wanted to be treated with respect and dignity, but it took some time and Rob and I made peace with the likelihood that I would be dismissed.

On the day of the outcome, my lawyer advised me to go to the office first and take all my personal belongings and leave them in my car because my MD would want to humiliate me by walking me to my desk in front of everyone to clear my desk and watch over me like a criminal. He was of the view that to avoid that humiliation, I would rather go do it myself, and I heeded his advice. I cleared my drawers, deleted all personal stuff from my PC, and took my pictures and everything that belonged to me.

Everyone in the office looked at me as if they knew I would be dismissed and looked surprised when I emptied out my stuff. I took my belongings to the car, sat in the car, had a good cry, and said to God, "Just give me strength to get through this meeting without a tear." I went to the meeting and I was dismissed. I completed all my exit documents and the same weak and scared HR person said to me, "I will walk you to your desk to clear your personal stuff," but the MD jumped in and said, "No, I will. I want to make sure she takes everything." My response was, I had already done that and would see her at the CCMA. They both stood there pale, and I walked out smiling. I broke down in the car even though I had known it was coming. It was so hard to hear it. I was dismissed on Valentine's Day in 2018.

Thereafter, we appointed an attorney for the matter. He was way more experienced in this field; we were referred to him by the lawyer who had assisted me initially. They were friends. I tell you God's hand was in this from the beginning. The first meeting at the CCMA was to try mediate; no attorneys allowed, but I was scripted on what to say.

The company did not send the weak, scared HR girl; they sent someone that I had never met before. I told the commissioner I would like to go to arbitration. I got my date for the arbitration, which was sent to the company. Not only that, I had over 455 pages of evidence against the company; I had a whole file, which I handed to my attorney. He and I met once. He needed clarity and told me that on the day of my arbitration, I should simply keep quiet; he would talk.

On the day that is exactly what I did and suddenly the company asked to settle. They did not want the matter to go to arbitration and that is because they knew I had a strong case against them. The meeting was adjourned and I called Rob first to let him know and he said it was up to me; he would support me either way. I told him I could go on with arbitration, which could go for months but I was tired. I was physically, mentally, and emotionally drained. These people had already taken too much from me and it was not good for our children. He said as long as I was happy and was paid what I deserved, I could accept the settlement. I then called the lawyer friend of ours and he said it's fine to settle, but I needed to make sure they did not try to cheat me or short change me in any way. He advised that if I was not happy with what they were offering, I should continue with arbitration.

The amount was settled. I was not wavering or negotiating. They were not happy, but they agreed to pay me out. The battle was over. I stood even though I had been knocked out a few times. I got some heavy blows and suffered some sucker punches, but it was all over. I cried that day and just said, "Thank you, Jesus. Your hand was in this all the way even down to the people that were sent to help me. Thank you for allowing me to see this demon through once and for all."

Today, the MD does not own the company any more. She is an employee. The non-white staff now have permanent contracts and enjoy benefits they were not entitled to before. The spotlight was placed on this issue and there are no more privileges for the white race. Everyone has fair and flexible working hours, all because one person decided to take a stand to fight and to not give up.

All I wanted was to be treated fairly, with respect and dignity. That was it, but I was asking for too much. The company put me through the cover-ups, lies, coercing, and forging of signatures and documents. I now understand what corporate espionage is; probably not what you think of when you hear the word "spy". It's not Sean Connery with his debonair manner, nor is it Tom Cruise hanging from a suspension cable. Sometimes it's as simple as a woman dressed up in her corporate attire, sitting in front of a computer with her guns out for you.

I believe Apartheid is still very much alive and healthy in the corporate space.

Lessons Learnt

- Even those people who say they know Christ will stab you in the back and lie about you.
- Never stop standing up for what you believe in, even if it means sometimes you have to stand alone.
- Your morals, principles, and values should never be wavered; they should be deeply grounded regardless of what comes.

Defining

Track 11

Oh, Lord! You're Beautiful

Your face is all I seek,
And when your eyes are on this child,
Your grace abounds to me.
Oh Lord, you're beautiful,
Your face is all I seek,
And when your eyes are on this child,
Your grace abounds to me.
I want to take your word and shine it all around. First help me
just to live it Lord.
And when I'm doing well, help me to never seek a crown.
For my reward is bringing glory to you.

SONG BY JESUS CULTURE

CHAPTER 11
Mom

As you know by now, I didn't have much of a mother-daughter relationship with my mother for years. We just could never seem to find common ground; we could never cultivate that bond. I always tried to mend fences because for the longest time, I felt that I needed my mother. I had a need. I needed a mother. That is what is considered normal, right? Well that's what I thought and as a result, I over-looked many of her shortcomings and faults not realising how unhealthy that was for me, my marriage, and my children.

For years, I did what I call "the washing machine cycle" with my mother and my family. We kept doing the same thing over and over just like a washing machine. We had this roller-coaster ride of a relationship and I took my husband and children on this ride every time. It was a volatile and unhealthy journey. We would be good for a month or two then suddenly, we would not talk for a couple of months. We never sat down and dealt with the problem that might have caused the breakdown and as a result of this, we would find ourselves in the same boat months down the line. Little did I know that God had to get rid of my stumbling blocks.

Late 2017, my mother and sister found themselves in a position where they needed mine and Rob's help. We took them both and my nephew in. They were both unemployed at the time, so we tried to make the situation slightly better for them. We let our daughters give up their bedroom, and they were sleeping in our bedroom on the floor some nights and other nights Rob and I would let them sleep on our bed, while we took the floor. A couple of weeks later, Rob got my sister a job, and she was so happy, but for some reason, my mother just never seemed happy. No matter what we did or tried to do, she just never seemed happy. We took care of everyone, which was not easy, but God knows, we tried our best. We did our best with what we had but at no point was anyone taking care of us or at least me, nothing like a simple: "How are you doing?" "Are you ok?" It all felt like, "you took us in so take care of us". I never felt a sincere sense of gratitude nor did I feel like we were living together trying to help each other because we are family.

Months went by and in the beginning things were fine, but slowly things started to unravel. My mother started being mean to my kids; she started buying things and hiding them. Now this was not a first for us because we had lived with my mother before and this is what she would do, but my children started picking up on her meanness and hiding of stuff to a point where she would not even want to give them. Now to me, these are kids, her grandchildren; I couldn't understand, but I had to see and realise that the way my mother felt about me manifested in her relationship with my husband and children. I always wondered why she wouldn't want to do better with my children. I would talk to her and ask her why she was hiding things from my children because when we bought things no one was excluded. We took care of everyone, so why was it so difficult for her to do the same? Now, at this point I realised that my mother did not take kindly to confrontation, whether it was calm and collected or volatile. Things started unravelling where I would somehow walk in-to her telephonic conversations with my siblings in which Rob and I were the subject. She would tell how unhappy she was, how she just wanted to leave, how horrible we were to her, and again, I would ask her why she was having untruthful conversations ab-out us and what was happening. She would blow it up and walk out.

28th March 2018, weeks and months went by with emotions building up from mine and Rob's side. The disrespect and disregard just grew and grew and on this day, we had our third iron break in just three months and I asked our helper at the time and my mother about it because they were the only two people who were using the iron. My helper tried to explain and my mother simply took that as her opportunity to offload thirty years of emotions and pain. Just before the offload session, Rob had called me and when we were done, I didn't drop his call, and he stayed on the line and heard every word of the conversation or the "explosion".

I told my mother that she was never a mother to me and she had caused a lot of my pain; that she always made me believe I was not good enough for anything; that she made me think I was second best and I wouldn't allow her to make my children feel that way; and that she would never see me and my children ever again. I told her that she made us choose as kids between her and my father, which was completely unfair because we should not have been involved in their fights and that I blame her for my father leaving us. She was never a nice person to us at home, and never happy at home. My mother stood there and said to me, "I never liked you." She said I was a horrible and miserable human being, a terrible mother and an even worse wife to a useless man. The last three things I heard my mother say to me were:

- I am nothing but a prostitute;
- I will amount to nothing; and
- My sister is far better than me.

I asked my mother to leave my house and told her that I was done. I left to go and audition for a TV commercial. I cried all the way there, the words that pierced my soul were: "I never liked you". As much as those words cut me deep, they made sense. My childhood finally made sense. My mother did what she did because she didn't like me. Now I can never imagine telling my kids that I don't like them, but I had to process and deal with this. It took me well over a year-and-a-half to deal with it. By God's grace, I have dealt with it and today, three years on, I can talk about it without crying.

I am happy and content living my life without my family, without a mother even though she is alive and well. I cannot hate her for telling her truth; I forgive her and pray that she comes to a point in her life where she takes accountability and responsibility for her actions. Not only that, I have made peace with the fact that I will probably never get an apology from her and that is ok with me. Furthermore, I am at peace and that only happens when you allow yourself to deal with things.

In these three years, I have seen my mother three times and all I've said is "Hi" and "Bye". I have heard many untrue and ugly stories my mother has gone and told people about me, and it doesn't faze me because I know who I am and have no desire to keep telling my side of the story. People can believe what they choose to believe. I am at peace.

We have no relationship and there is no relationship between my mother and my children. I deserve better and so do my children. No one will ever make my children feel as if they are not good enough or second best.

My mother and I will only talk again when she is ready to apologise to me and take accountability and responsibility for her actions toward me as my mother. Until then, I am at peace and will continue to live my purpose. My mother's feelings toward me cannot stop me from living; I have to live for me and for my children. I choose to drop my childhood batons and to do better.

Bonus Track

If I Was Only Welcomed In

I would be so honored
There's so much to tell you
My love I give to make it better
If I was only welcomed in
I could take this sorrow
Replace it all with laughter,
it's true
I have so much to show you
If I was only welcomed in
If I was only welcomed in
The promise I would keep
If I was only welcomed in
These persons I will be
A friend, a help, a scholar
If I was only welcomed in

SONG BY BEBE & CECE WINANS

Lessons Learnt

• Sometimes it's our own flesh and blood that the devil uses to break us. Our very own which will cause us pain and block our blessings. I refuse for anyone to block my blessings, if peace is not what you're offering then I do not need you in my space. This decision taught me to protect my space and if it means my family will be put on the back burner, then I am not doing it.
• I cannot help others, even family, at the expense of my own family.
• If God doesn't tell me to do something, I am not going to do it. Gone are the days of making emotional decisions.

To every woman, wife and mom, you can stop the cycle and change your outcome; it's never too late.

Track 12

In Harm's Way

Undying love you've given to me
Seen in me things I would never have seen
I don't understand why you care so much, it's all a mystery
Time and time again I ask myself
What have I done to deserve such wealth
The price you paid, I could never repay your generosity
In wanting to save me
In order to save the day
Because of love you placed yourself
In harm's way

SONG BY BEBE WINANS

CHAPTER 12

Dad

My dad was around but not a present dad and never spoke much. I guess when I listen to how he was raised, I understand his personality. He was always alone since the age of thirteen, so having relationships and knowing how to build and mend them is something he was not taught.

I don't know much about my father and his family; when I was a child I would ask but never got answers. What I do know is that he always did things for people, always helped people in church and outside without any misgiving. However, at home he just never seemed happy and that's why I guess, the older I got, the less I remember him being home and even sleeping at home. He and my mother were married, but I don't think they ever had a marriage. That filtered down to us as children; we weren't taught how to be a family or how to have each other's backs because our parents didn't have each other's backs. We lost a lot growing up because of decisions made by both my parents, whether it was turning a blind eye or simply doing as they pleased. As the children, those decisions made us suffer greatly.

My parents' marriage was tested time after time, but I guess at the end of 2007, the real test came. One morning, my dad handed my younger sister a R10 note and said goodbye. He left, as in took all his belongings and left. He changed his number and was gone; we had no idea what happened or where he had gone or even if he was alive. My mother told us that he had left because he never wanted any of us. We didn't have a family meeting to discuss or talk; we only held on to what we were told and that was it.

Months later, he called as if nothing had happened and said he was fine. When we asked where he was, he would tell us that he was fine and laughed. He would give each of us different answers when we asked where he was, so we never really knew where exactly he was. We would make arrangements with him to meet but on the day of the planned meeting, his phone would be off and no one could get hold of him for weeks thereafter. Then he would call again and not talk about what happened. I realised my dad also did not like to deal with problems or be confronted or asked about his flaws. I stopped reaching out and calling. I just felt that I could not chase someone who didn't want to be found. I also noticed that he felt he did not owe anyone an explanation regarding his sudden departure from our lives. He would call me now and then just to ask how I was and to say hi. Those were our conversations for over six years. I still continued to pray for him and for God to make a way for him to come home before he passed on.

In 2009, he was diagnosed with cancer, he called one of us to tell us years later when it got worse. Still he didn't want to give us information about where he was, which hospital he was in. We felt he would call if he wanted us to know. The cancer got worse over the years and when he was no longer strong enough to look after himself, he called saying he was ready to come back.

Rob and I fetched him in November 2019, and we then found out from his doctor's visits that he has prostate cancer and the cancer is in stage four. My dad has three other children outside his marriage to my mother. I met them in December 2019 when we invited everyone over to see him. The family was so welcoming and so supportive during that visit; I even encouraged my dad to sit his children down and apologise to them for the wrongs he has done to them because at the end of the day, he is old and sick; we cannot go back and change anything. All he can do is apologise and hope for better relationships, which he did.

16+ months of having my dad, Rob and I solely take care of my dad. We make sure he gets to his weekly doctor's visits, gets his monthly medication and see to his daily needs. Since my dad came to us, not one of his children has ever fetched him to take him for a coffee or a breakfast. They invite him over when they're having functions and parties, but never a one-on-one to check up on him. Before, Rob and I would ask for help; some would help as long as they weren't inconvenienced, or we would either get excuses or we would simply be ignored. Now, we don't ask for anything. We just do, tag-team and get things done. Some days are hard because we have so much to do and also bearing in mind we have no support structure, we are our own support structure when it comes to our family. Can you imagine knowing you have stage four cancer and the doctor says it's likely for you to go to bed and not wake up, but your children do not make a plan to spend quality time with you? Rob and I try our utmost best, but there is also only so much we can do.

With my family it is always bad-mouthing and gossiping about each other. Because I have no relationship with my family, we always seem to be the topic of discussion but no one takes into account what we do for my dad every day. There is no inkling of gratitude or support; it's just always having something bad to say and looking for stories, instead of focusing on his health and making sure he is ok. Had Rob and I not fetched my dad the day we did, my dad would have passed on the very next day or week because of complications with his catheter. This is what the doctor told us when we rushed him to the hospital.

While my dad has been with me, we get to talk a lot and I get to see and understand his perspective about things; a story really has three sides. For the longest time, my mother got to tell her story and that's the story that has stuck because you hear it so often.

Then when you hear my dad's side, a very different side, you realise that my parents are two broken people who never healed but you can't help people who do not see a problem.

Lessons Learnt

• Don't build your life based on one side of the story; do
yourself a favour and hear both sides, then make a decision.
• We will all get old and how we treat the old folk will come
back and find us. What we sow, we will reap.
• I am a student of life and life has the ability to teach you
things.

Track 13

Didn't Know My Own Strength

Lost touch with my soul. I had nowhere to turn. I had nowhere to go. Lost sight of my dream. Thought it would be the end of me. I thought I'd never make it through. I had no hope to hold on to, I thought I would break. I didn't know my own strength. And I crashed down, and I tumbled but I did not crumble. I got through all the pain

SONG BY WHITNEY HOUSTON

CHAPTER 13

Light Bulb Moment

In my twenties, I was completely lost. I was in a dark place and just as the song says, I thought it would be the end of me; I thought I'd never make it through. I got through the pain and when the pain subsided, the light bulb went on.

At twenty-nine and a half, I decided that it was time; it was time to start living and stop existing. I told myself it's time to find me. I had had enough of the darkness and pain. Something had to give. I refused to have another decade pass me by. One day I said to Rob, "Soon I am turning thirty and I refuse to live and feel the way I did in my twenties. In my thirties I don't want anything or any person that brought me pain and was not good to me." I decided that I wanted to find me, live life, build myself, and enjoy my children. I became intentional about my life.

This was a hard process because at times you have to face some ugly truths about yourself, but the journey to meeting Semonia Maureen Phillips began.

At the age of thirty, I met myself. I had a reintroduction to meet me. I actually liked her. She was a diamond covered with tons of pain, sadness, and aloneness, but once all that was dusted off, the diamond started to shine bit by bit. As I went through this journey, I began to realise that I had actually been a doormat for other people, that I was a "Yes" person; I could never say "No" to people, and it didn't matter at whose expense that was, at times it was mine and my family's. I was so dysfunctional; dysfunctional in my thinking, in my daily functions, to my core, and my DNA. I had to turn everything upside-down, and I mean everything. Allow me to be deliberate for a second.

What does it mean to be dysfunctional?

The term dysfunctional is defined as "abnormal or impaired functioning" on the part of an individual person, between people in any sort of relationship, or amongst members of a family. That was me, my living or mere existence was abnormal.

When on my self-discovery journey, one of the questions that kept coming up was: What batons am I handing over to my children? I didn't like the answers that came up and no one could change that except me. When you become intentional about yourself, about your own healing, you have to go back to the beginning, that is, your childhood because that is where you began. I had to be intentional about my healing and by being intentional I had to deal with childhood pain, childhood rejection, and childhood trauma that was placed on me. I, too, had to deal with these batons.

How did I deal with these? It was not an easy journey. At times I felt as if I was ripped open, but I had to do it for myself and most importantly for my children. I do not want my children and my grandchildren walking around with my childhood batons. Not only that, I had to start by telling myself that I was not at fault. It was nothing I did wrong; I was just a child. During my journey, I realised that my parents projected their own childhood pain and rejection onto me.

I started off by telling myself that it was not my fault, and it was not mine to carry and most importantly, I needed to release this and give it back to my parents by having conversations with them. I released it all and gave it back to them not because I needed an apology or because I needed them to feel bad, but purely for me. I needed release for me, for my well-being and that of my marriage, and my children. Releasing my pain was a very crucial step for me in my journey. It was a huge part of my healing process.

I had to tell my parents how they made me feel as a child, the pain and traumas they had passed onto me and how that made me feel as a child. I had to tell them that when they dropped the ball as my parents, I was impacted. I had to open up and let them know so that I could be free and so that my children would not suffer as a result of my childhood traumas. My parents also did not realise that they had passed on their childhood pain and traumas onto me; they did it unknowingly. However, once we know better, we need to do better. The more the journey continued, the more determined I became not to hand over a baton of pain, of trauma, and of rejection to my children.

Lessons Learnt

- Our adult drama stems from our childhood trauma.
- Healing is a hard thing to go through. Sometimes we need to have hard, uncomfortable, and brutally honest conversations with ourselves and others.
- Healing is probably the messiest, the most uncomfortable, and the ugliest journey ever that any human being can go through and it's only a few that actually allow themselves to go through it.

Track 14

I'm Gonna Be Ready

Sight beyond what I see, You know what's best for me. Prepare my mind, prepare my heart for whatever comes, I'm gonna' be ready. Strength to pass any test, I feel like I'm so blessed with You in control, I can't go wrong, Cause I always know. I'm gonna be ready. I was free to do what I wanted to, lost everything, but I still had You. You showed me your grace now my life's renewed and I thank You (yes. I thank You). So I'll tell anyone who'll listen, I'll testify about how good You were to me when so call friends passed me by. The fact that You would show somebody so broke down so much mercy.

SONG BY YOLANDA ADAMS

CHAPTER 14

I Will Continue

Oh! But trust me, the freedom that comes thereafter is incredible; I felt so much lighter and free. The healing and dealing process is extremely hard; I had to make a conscious decision and be intentional about my healing.

My children pushed me to want to do better; to be better. I had to make sure I did right by them, but it started with me. All this had to start with me; I learnt that my children didn't need a perfect mother. They needed a healthy and happy one, and I had to work on me, as painful as some days were, for them; I had to push through. I had to push through all the hurt and pain so that I could be a healthy, happy mom; one that handed over healthy batons to them.

Speaking about batons, looking back at my childhood, I had a lot of my parents' batons handed over to me, and as a child, I didn't realise that I carried these batons with me into adulthood, into my relationships whether it was good or bad. You subconsciously carry them with you. Now, as a child, there isn't much you can do about the different batons handed to you, but as an adult you have a choice to continue carrying these batons of hurt and trauma with you and as a result you hand this over to your children and the cycle simply continues. Let me ask. What hurtful and painful batons were handed to you as a child? What batons do you still carry today, or every day, whether willingly or unwillingly? During this journey, I discovered that as an adult, you now have an option to do better by yourself, and for your children. I, too, had to deal with these batons.

I dealt with these by being intentional about my healing and by being intentional I had to deal with childhood pain, childhood rejection, and childhood trauma placed on me, and it was not an easy journey. At times I felt as if I was ripped open, but I had to do it for myself and most importantly for my children. I do not want my children and my grandchildren walking around with my childhood pain batons. I had to start by telling myself that it was not me. It was nothing I did wrong; I was just a child.
Dealing with stuff was hard, it was gut-wrenching at times, but I had to, for me. It was easy to default back to the so-called "normal" but I pushed forward because I was worth it.

You need to get to a point in your life where you are able to let people know how they make you feel; good or bad. We need to be able to release and deal with things because we cannot go through life bottling things up, because one day we might just have this massive explosion because of built-up emotions. Let people know how you feel and leave it there, don't walk around with others' emotions; we cannot manage people's emotions at our expense. Release and let it go; give it back to whomever it may belong to.

Now one of the greatest gifts God has given us is the power to choose. In fact, every day, we are faced with hundreds of decisions. We decide whether to get out of bed, what we'll eat, what we'll do, what we will think about, and what we will say. We make decisions about everything, from how we style our hair to how we will react to more serious situations in our lives.

In Deuteronomy 30:19 God says, "I have set before you life and death, the blessings and the curses; therefore, choose life that you and your descendants may live."

It is important to understand that every choice we make is a seed we sow and those seeds produce fruits in our lives — either for life or death. So if we want to have the life Jesus died to give us — an abundant life full of peace and joy — then we need to make wise choices.

So to me, it became simple and crystal clear. Good choices lead to a good life, which meant everything had to change; my thinking, what I was taught as a child, what I learned along the way; everything had to change. It started with my thinking. This was not an easy journey because I permitted myself to start my life chapter over. It is never too late. No one has the right to give and to take away anything from you. Allow yourself to start over. If you don't like where you are, change it.

Give yourself permission to reset your life, press that red button and reset things.

Once I could release the painful triggers and actually deal with them one by one, I realised that I had no boundaries, I was a doormat for people, and I needed to change that. Now once you start implementing boundaries, it is frowned upon because people are so used to you doing things a certain way for years and suddenly you are not. Some will suggest that you are rude, that you have changed into some-one that they don't recognise or like. Just remember that boundaries are healthy and not everyone will appreciate them, but stick to your guns and keep pushing through, soon you will see the benefits. I had to learn to say "No" without a reason. I had to learn to think about things before answering. I had to understand who was actually good for me and who was not, who had my best interests at heart and who was simply using me.

Allow me to be deliberate:

What do we mean by boundaries? Something (such as a river, a fence, or an imaginary line) that shows where an area ends and another begins. A point or limit that indicates where two things become differ-rent. Unofficial rules about what should not be done; limits that define acceptable behaviour.

I love the last part, "limits that define acceptable be-haviour". The beauty about boundaries is that you decide what acceptable behaviour is and what is not.
Now allow me to define "relationship boundaries"? Boundaries refer to limits that you put in place to protect your well-being. When boundaries are clearly communicated, along with the consequences for breaking them, your partner understands your expectations. It is all about your well-being, therefore, I had to create solid and non-negotiable boundaries. It was not about other people, but it was about me. Finding me was about creating a new functional and healthy life.

At the age of thirty-two, I was starting to find me and found out what I liked and what I didn't and funny enough, tattoos were one of the things I actually liked because I grew up being taught that tattoos were evil and that having them was a sin. I got my very first one at thirty-two, which was the initials of our children – KEMZE – and by finding and meeting myself, I realised that I really liked the form of art; it was my way of expressing myself. Well the journey has continued, and I absolutely love it. I am free to express myself and it is for me, not for anyone else.

As the process continued, I started finding my voice. Remember at the age of thirty-four I was fired and that entire experience allowed me to find my voice, my inner strength, and allowed me to discover parts of me which I didn't even know existed. I realised I had the ability to be persistent and relentless in what I wanted and what I truly believed in. Sometimes we hold on to things so tight not realising that letting go will bring us our greatest blessings. For the longest time my thinking was: our household needed two incomes for us to survive and I held on to being employed, held on to having an access card and having an employee number, but that was not my purpose. I believe if I was not fired, I would probably still be an unhappy employee, but that needed to happen to me for me to find my purpose and discover my greatest blessings. This book probably would never have become a reality because I would not have had the self-belief and confidence to write it.

I turned upside-down, inside-out, everything that I was taught, everything I learnt, everything I was exposed to, everything I thought was right or wrong, and everything that allowed me to function or not function. I had to. I simply refused to continue living a dysfunctional life and I was not going to hand over dysfunctional batons to my children. It all stopped with me, family dysfunction, generational curses, and deep rooted unresolved pains and hurts.

The more the journey continued, I refused to hand over a baton of pain, of trauma, and of rejection to my children. I had to make a conscious decision and be intentional about my healing. Healing is a hard thing to go through. Sometimes we need to have hard, uncomfortable and brutally honest conversations with ourselves and others. Oh! Trust me, the freedom that comes thereafter is incredible; I felt so much lighter and free. The process is extremely hard, but once you get to the end, you look back and say, "It was worth it."

Today, I simply want to say, if you have been handed a baton of pain, rejection or trauma, whether it is from your childhood or past or present relationships, don't let it continue. It is not too late to drop that baton, stop the race and take time to heal, you must deal with it so that it does not become a trigger in your life. Deal with everything, every bit of emotion because at the end of the day you are worth it, you are worthy of a life of peace and freedom and your children deserve only good batons handed over to them.

Facing my greatest pain points was extremely hard, but I had to because I deserved better irrespective of who thought or said what. I deserved better because had I continued these pain points, they would have eventually turned into triggers, and anyone who triggered that pain would have to deal with the volcanic eruption which would follow because I did not heal. Dealing with stuff was hard, it was gut-wrenching at times, but I had to, for me.

Now I see how the devil tried to crush and break me from all angles in my twenties because he knew what was going to happen in my thirties, he knew I would be able to walk in my purpose and become a force. It is never too late to find you; it is never too late to give yourself permission to reset, and it is never too late to take your power back and become the force you have been destined to be.

I am seven years into my self-discovery journey and every day I still wake up being intentional about me. I am far from perfect, perfection is not something I strive for; I simply want to be unapologetic, authentic, and real to myself. I strive to be able to share my story and journey and hope to be able to inspire, impact and give to someone. God has blessed me with incredible opportunities which I am so grateful for. Seven years ago, I did not think that I would be featured in international magazines, international blogs, let alone write a book. I just thought I would be another employee, with a new employee number, but my dismissal notice broke chains and limitations I had. Don't ever disregard your season, you never know what lies behind it. Who would have thought that after all my tears I would sit and thank God for allowing me to be dismissed, yet here I am with absolute and constant gratitude flowing from my veins.

I love myself, flaws and all, imperfections and all, good and bad days. I am confident in myself and have come to understand who I am and what I have been designed to do. Now it is very difficult to break someone who knows who they are, who does not carry past pains, who does not need the validation of people and who simply stands in their truth.

Remember, happiness is you; you are your own happiness. Your inner peace should be the most valuable possession you have and don't allow anyone to interfere with that peace. Your peace must be something that you should not compromise, ever. Not for anyone.

The steps/tools I used to become intentional:

1. Isolate yourself
2. Shut out the noise
3. Spend time with yourself
4. Find out who you are, what you like
5. Deal with past and present pain and traumas
6. Create boundaries
7. Find your voice and don't be afraid to use it
8. Be patient with yourself
9. Be gentle with yourself
10. Accept yourself, flaws and all
11. Be aware of self
12. Be happy with yourself
13. Be at peace with yourself

I don't know what is next for me, but believe I'm gonna be ready.

To every person who has helped us on our journey, a heartfelt "Thank you". To those who helped because you were being obedient to the Holy Spirit, may you be blessed beyond your measure. Those who saw a need and helped out of the goodness of your heart, may your cup continue to overflow. I am so grateful for the journey I have walked and continue to walk.
I will never be ashamed of where I come from, and I never want to forget where I come from.

To every woman reading this book, allow me to be testament that it is never too late to press "reset", to find you, and to live your purpose.

Give yourself permission to find you and to live. Stop existing and start living. You deserve it.

Stay present in your presence. Stay Inspired to Inspire. - *Simone Phillips*

Lessons Learnt from 11 Years of Nappies

- I get to choose the life I want to live. I get to choose the woman, wife and mother I am.
- My past, my upbringing, and my DNA do not get to define who I am. I do.
- It's not how your start but how it ends.
- I am enough and I am worthy of every good thing this life has to offer.
- It's never too late; give yourself the permission to reset your life.

Live | Learn | Repeat...